'If you want to go on a great adven
Geoff takes you on a rollercoaster hi
60s' London music scene, then off
where his life took a dramatic turn. C
him in the Himalayan kingdom of N ___ ____ ___ ____ ___ valuable
faith lessons in trusting God for everything. Miracles abound around
every corner. A book to draw you in to amazing adventures. You
won't be able to put it down.'

Barry Manson, international speaker and author,
High Voltage Ministry

'I've known Geoff since one of his returns to the UK mentioned in
his book *Finding Faith in Unexpected Places* – first as a guest speaker,
then missions pastor, pastor and friend. The experiences he shares
have filled a lot of gaps in what I already knew to be a truly amazing
journey. Geoff's faith is summarised in one sentence: *"I was determined to follow him whatever the consequences."* The results of this
attitude have rippled across Northern India and Nepal for more than
thirty years and I'm sure we will never know this side of heaven how
many lives have been added to God's Kingdom because of it. I believe this book should be required reading in Bible schools and recommended to anyone who senses mission work to be in their future.'

Stephen Chaudhary, Pastor,
River of Life Christian Centre, Bristol

'Geoff Walvin is the real deal and his book *Finding Faith in Unexpected
Places* reads like the book of Acts is still being written. In it you will
see how God takes a brand new convert who dedicates himself to following the Lord 'whatever the consequences' and uses him to reach
the unreached with the gospel of Jesus Christ. Geoff's writing takes
you to places most of us have only heard of; you will see the sights,
hear the sounds, and sense the atmosphere. You will also learn how,
through simple trust, God will guide you in the decisions you need
to make, and provide for you every step of the way. This book will
inspire and encourage you – it did me!'

Aaron Chaudhary, Pastor, New Generation Church,
Newton Aycliffe, UK

'I first met Geoff Walvin thirty-five years ago at a church I was serving in. We had a mutual friend who was a missionary in Nepal. I did not realise then or for many years the incredible life he has lived. He has taken the gospel to the most remote places on the planet, and discovered the miraculous provision of God in some of the most unusual places. His quiet, determined personality has had a hidden apostolic gift and as a result he instigated church planting movements, raising leaders with a national influence. I am delighted that God's story in his life is captured in the book. You will be blessed and ignited to live a life of radical obedience and faith. Then watch God work through you and see his kingdom come.'

Ian Green, Pioneer, Speaker, Consultant,
Coach and Author

'Everyone has a story to tell that is filled with experiences that add value and create lasting memories. I have known Geoff for close to thirty years and thought that in this book his passion and life's purpose is clearly seen. I have heard Geoff tell some of his experiences from places like India and his eyes and face always beam with enthusiasm and excitement. This book captures a lot of Geoff's experiences of what God can do when someone says yes to the adventure. I trust that it will inspire others to live the kind of life that looks to serve others.'

Mark Wilkinson, Lead Pastor,
Hillsong Church, Berlin, Germany

Finding Faith in Unexpected Places

How a spiritual awakening on the hippy trail led to sharing God's love in Nepal

Geoff Walvin

Authentic

First published 2022 by Authentic Media Limited,
PO Box 6326, Bletchley, Milton Keynes, MK1 9GG.
authenticmedia.co.uk

British Library Cataloguing in Publication Data
A catalogue record for this book is available from the British Library.
ISBN: 978-1-78893-226-4
978-1-78893-227-1 (e-book)

Cover design by Jennifer Burrell, Fresh Vision Design
Printed and bound by CPI Group (UK) Ltd, Croydon, CR0 4YY

Dedication

For my parents

Acknowledgements

I'd like to thank my wife, June, and daughters Laura and Amy for their constant support and encouragement in writing this book. Thank you, June, for releasing me to spend long hours shut in a room to write and for encouraging me to keep going. Thank you, Laura and Amy, for encouraging me to write the stories I have been sharing with you over the years. You are amazing and I love you all so much.

I'd like to thank those who are mentioned within these pages. My brother Colin, Sally and the late Floyd McClung, Dave and Angie Andrews, Steve and Kathy Aram, Claude and Indira Barua, Dilip Chhetri (not forgetting Meena!), and Connie Ong (not forgetting Daniel!). Thank you, Connie, for the push to write the book and submit it to a publisher. First of all, I'd like to thank each of you for giving me permission to include you in the book and secondly, the reason why you are in it is because each of you have played a major role in the story of my life as told in these pages. Thank you.

There are so many other people I would like to thank but there are too many names to mention. Thank you to all of my friends, far and wide, who have been a major part of my life. Each of you are like threads which have been woven into the tapestry that my life has become. You know who you are and I appreciate you.

A special thanks goes to all those who have written endorsements. Thank you so much.

And last, but not least, a very special thanks must go to the team at Authentic Media for taking on my book. Thank you so much for your hard work, constant support, guidance and advice and for always being there when I needed to know what to do next. You have all been amazing.

Contents

1

Changing Times

The warm afternoon sun kissed the earth. Nothing could be heard except the faint rustle of leaves as they were touched by a gentle breeze blowing through the trees and across the valley. The dry, ochre-coloured earthen floor on which I lay was warm and sun-baked. I breathed in the pure mountain air, which was infused with the gentle fragrance of parched earth mixed with fir and pine. As the sun began its descent beyond the Himalayan mountains, I watched the shadows fill the valley and thanked God for this place of refuge on the veranda of this simple Nepalese home.

The nausea, stomach cramps and vomiting I had experienced earlier, while trekking the Himalayan trail, had abated somewhat, but I still felt too weak to continue. After two days of walking from Kathmandu, I had become so increasingly sick and exhausted that all I could do was lie there. I had no energy to go on. The two Nepalese friends I was travelling with had left me in the care of a family in this mountain home. They had gone on to establish things in the Sherpa village we would be visiting and would come back to get me the next morning.

As I lay on the dried, mud floor I covered my face with the edge of a thin, dark-coloured sarong to protect my eyes from the glaring rays of the sun. The sun was beginning to set and a coolness descended upon the valley. Suddenly the silence was broken by the slow, soft sound of bare feet upon clay earth moving in my direction. The shaman stood before me. Without moving he looked directly at me as I lay on the floor alone, sick and helpless.

Suddenly the silence broke. Strange, hissing incantations came from his mouth. His body began to tremble. He began to sway back and forth and entered into a trance-like state. His voice increased in volume and the chanting words that came from his mouth increased in speed. He raised both hands in front of me. In one hand he held a sacrificial metal bowl, which was used in religious rituals, and in the other hand, sharp and menacing, was a long, silver knife. My heart quickened its beat as the atmosphere became increasingly tinged with a dark, foreboding presence. I felt fear rise inside. My breathing became constricted as I lay perfectly still. Placing the knife into the bowl he began to beat the sides of the metal making a loud clanging noise. His voice, and the sound of the knife beating against the bowl, increased in volume and speed as he began to tremble.

My mind filled with thoughts of what could happen next. I felt a strong fear rise within me as I focused on images of what could be the worst possible outcome. On the one hand I knew that his intention may not be to harm me but I could not help thinking of the horrendous stories I had heard over recent months of tourists who had been brutally murdered around Kathmandu and the surrounding mountains. It was later discovered that two of these were victims of the infamous serial killer Charles Sobhraj. His story, as highlighted in the BBC drama series *The Serpent*, follows his path of brutal, gruesome murders along the hippy trail which led him to Nepal. Messages had been posted in embassies and major tourist spots warning people to be cautious and not to travel into the mountains alone. I now found myself alone, sick and helpless with no other protection except from God himself. I didn't know if the person in front of me was there to try to bring healing to my sick body through some form of Hindu or Buddhist ritual, or could it be possible that I would be the next victim? I wasn't sure.

Eventually, as moments passed, his voice softened into silence and his arms relaxed as he stopped beating the metal bowl with the knife. As softly as he came, his footsteps moved away from me and his form disappeared. I knew then that I was safe and that he had offered a Buddhist prayer for my healing. There were no doctors or medicine where he lived. He had a kind heart and only knew to do what generations had done before him in time-honoured rituals. Although I now felt safe, and at peace, this experience had been one mixed with fear and apprehension. Faced with what could have possibly been death, images and memories of my life had passed before me and I thought of events that had happened over the years, events that had led me on a journey of amazing adventures and daring faith into some of the world's most incredible places. That journey began on a cold October evening on the outskirts of London. This is my story.

I stood at the side of the road leading out of London and faced oncoming vehicles. In the internationally known hitchhikers' expression, my arm was stretched out towards the road with my thumb pointing in the direction I was planning to travel. The sun had set beyond the city skyline and, although still early evening, it was cold, damp and dark with the beginnings of a London fog. I was looking forward to the day when I would reach the edge of Asia and discard the heavy clothes I was now wearing in an attempt to stay warm. After spending several weeks on overland travel, my final destination would be India, that vast, distant, exotic land which filled my imagination with pictures of tropical jungles, barren deserts and ancient palaces. A land filled with temples and streets filled with vibrant colour and life.

This was 1972, when many young people hitchhiked around the country. Unlike today, hitchhiking was a safe way to travel and, of course, it was free. I had saved enough money to travel overland to India, but being on a tight budget I needed to make the money I had with me last. My plan to help with this was to begin by hitchhiking through France, Belgium, Germany, Austria, what was then Yugoslavia, and Bulgaria. Upon reaching the ancient city of Istanbul, I would travel by cheaper local transport through Turkey, across the deserts of Iran and Afghanistan, descend through the legendry Khyber Pass into Pakistan and eventually cross the border into the wild and exotic land that was India.

London was an incredible place to live at that time, and things had changed dramatically across the nation. This was the generation of baby boomers, those who were born after the war. I had grown up in the north-east of England in a solid, wonder-ful family, an only child until my brother was born when I was 12. My parents were born in the north-east of England in 1927 and grew up in the same community. Like many others, both of their fathers worked in the local coal-mining industry. Along with shipbuilding, coal mining was a major industry in this part of the UK and employed a large section of the population. In fact, whole communities depended on mining for their liveli-hood. Both of my grandfathers began work at age 14, working in horrendous conditions, for a paltry wage that was insufficient to provide a decent support for the whole family.

My dad was one of nine children and my mother one of four. My mother, along with her parents, two brothers and a sister, grew up in a small, two-bedroom house which had no heating except for one coal fire and a toilet which was detached from the house and was reached across an outside yard. There was no indoor bathroom and no hot running water. Fortunately, things were about to change for the better.

Like other men of his age, my dad was enlisted into the army at the end of the Second World War where he served in Palestine. On his return to England he met my mother, and they spent time working and meeting together with friends at local dances where they would jive to big band music and early rock and roll. This led to their marriage in 1950 and three years later, in 1953, I entered this world, their first child. The world I was born into was different from the one they had entered.

The war had changed everything. There were now opportunities their own parents had never experienced combined with a spirit of positivity across the nation. Along with that, there stirred a hope of building a better future – a future which, hopefully, would never see the horrors of what the UK had just been through over the previous years of war. This was time to build or, in some cases, to rebuild what had been destroyed.

It was also a time of major social reform and of building something different from the past. It seemed that, as the UK had survived the war, anything was possible. People worked hard; working and living conditions improved, giving people hope of a better life. Women, who had got used to working through the war, continued in employment outside the home, bringing in extra income for the family. Now there were two wages instead of one. Government initiatives brought about a higher standard of living which created suitable housing, free medical care, better educational systems and greater opportunities for people to get ahead in life.

In 1956 my parents moved into a new housing estate when I was 3 years old, and because many young families had also moved into the area, there were lots of children to play with. We actually had thirty children in our small street. Added to that, my wider family members mostly lived in the same community, so I had aunts, uncles and cousins everywhere. Needless to say, I never felt lonely. As children we had a great time, especially during school holidays, when we would head out for the day to explore and then return home in the evening. Our playground was open fields, woods, rivers, the sea, sand and nearby ancient ruins. In many ways it was a great life. We walked everywhere, including across fields each morning to reach school and then home again in the evening.

I have a vivid memory of one particular day at primary school. I was sitting at a desk at the front of the class. I think I was about 7 years old. The English teacher stood before us. I actually forget his name but still remember him very clearly. He was a small, wiry old school gentleman in a brown tweed suit with a gold-coloured watch and chain attached to his waist-coat. He always had immaculately polished brown shoes and had a wisp of grey hair. He reminded me of a character from a Dickens novel. 'Today,' he said, 'I want to introduce you to a special friend.' We all looked at him waiting for this special friend to appear when he held up a book. 'A book is my special friend, and he can be your special friend too. He can keep you company when you are alone and travel with you wherever you go. You can even travel the whole world and discover the most fascinating information and knowledge within his pages.'

So that fired me up to begin reading and ignited within me a love for books which has remained throughout my life. After school that day, and totally on my own initiative, I walked to the local library which, although only quite small, seemed enormously large to a small child. I walked up to the counter, barely able to see beyond it, as it was at my eye level. Towering above it was a lady librarian who looked down at me. She looked very official, and important, but had a kind face.

'Please, Miss,' I said. 'Can I join the library?'

'Of course you can,' she replied, and went on to tell me what I needed to do next. She then took me into the children's section and left me to browse the many shelves. I was amazed and felt that the whole world was at my fingertips. I read and read and read and discovered that there was a whole new, incredible world which lay outside our small community. My parents later invested in ten large volumes of an encyclopaedia and I read through them all. I travelled the whole world without leaving home. All of this ignited in me a passion at an early age to see the world and everything in it. I made the decision that one day I would travel the earth and live a life of adventure.

Summers were fun, and being a little older than most of the other children, I became a leader and would organise our summer adventures. Although we lived close to the city of Newcastle, our neighbourhood bordered on fields and woods which stretched out for several miles. We also lived just a short bus ride from the beach. Every day was a new adventure. Woods turned into mystical lands where we had to avoid mythical creatures and the beach became a place to search for hidden pirates' treasure. My grandmother lived in the house next door to us; unfortunately, as a part of one of my adventures I buried some of her costume jewellery, which I had decided was pirate's treasure, in her garden, and we could not find it later. It's probably still there today.

We were a new generation of children and different from previous generations in that, unlike the poverty experienced in the past, there was now more disposable income available per family. Our parents worked hard to make sure they could give us the best life possible. Money could be made and life could be great. Supermarkets opened, industry increased, people had a better income and the consumer society had arrived. Yet, with the focus on materialism and financial prosperity, there seemed to be a great spiritual void and a whole generation of young people entered early adulthood wondering if there was more to life than what our parents offered. I became one of those young people.

Holidays were a special time as each summer we would climb into the family car and head off to one of England's beach communities. This was always a special time and my dad would do everything he could to make it a great holiday. My parents enjoyed life and wherever we went they sought to live it to the full. Often other family members would join us and I would get to spend time with various cousins. I loved travelling, even at an early age.

By the time I entered my teens, a new change was coming to the nation, this time on a totally different scale. While the fifties, with its prosperity and economic boom, had brought a time of great transformation to the UK, the late sixties would bring further change, this time among young people. It felt like a revolution was brewing and I wanted to be a part of it.

In 1967 people of my parents and grandparents' generation thought the world of young people had gone crazy. This was the year of the Summer of Love. The hippy movement, which had been building momentum for some time, broke out in international news when more than 20,000 hippies congregated for an event in Golden Gate Park, San Francisco. Then around 100,000 hippies descended on San Francisco's Haight Ashbury district making it the capital of hippy culture and lifestyle. Like many other young people at that time, this caught my attention.

Suddenly, the UK newspapers were headlining stories of similar happenings in London and around the country. Things were changing and we were watching to see what would happen next as a whole new generation of young people began to rise up, challenging the status quo and believing they could change the world. In this season of psychedelia, men grew long hair and people wore colourful clothes, went barefoot, handed out flowers, talked about inner peace, world peace, love, freedom, spirituality and a new age that was about to dawn. Following this, Woodstock happened in the US when 400,000 people descended on Bethel, New York and hippy gatherings and music festivals like Glastonbury sprung up across the UK drawing large crowds.

Music always played a big role in propagating the new movement, and we all sang along with Bob Dylan and The Beatles as they sang about changing times and the world needing more love. Our parents had survived the Second World War, and the horrors of the Vietnam War, which had begun in 1955, were still hitting the news. It made sense to a lot of us that the world certainly could do with more love. I was still in my early teens, but something excited me about what was going on. This was a time of change, and I wanted to be a part of it.

London was where it was all happening. Major change was already stirring and everyone was talking about Carnaby Street and the King's Road, both centres of new fashion which broke with tradition and pushed boundaries. London was definitely the place to be. By the late sixties the Ladbroke Grove/Notting Hill area of London, which had previously been a community of beatniks and artists, was now becoming the UK's Haight Ashbury. From all across the country, young people who were attracted to the rising hippy movement arrived and settled into this area. Everything that was edgy and alternative was centred there.

In 1968 I visited London with some friends and stayed in an apartment just off the King's Road. Coming from a small northern community, I was amazed at how different life was. The King's Road was such a colourful, vibrant place. I immediately knew this was where I wanted to be. In the following year, believing life was too short and wanting to be a part of something bigger and more adventurous, I made the decision to leave the small community I had grown up in and head for the big city. Obviously, my parents didn't like the idea of me moving to London at such a young age, but I convinced them I would be OK. I bought a cheap overnight bus ticket and headed for London. I was 16 years old.

2

Spiritual Search

I arrived in London when the hippy movement was still at its peak. I found work in the retail sector and stayed with some friends until I was able to become more established and find my way forward. I loved being in the city of London with all that it offered. My goal was to live in the Notting Hill area, and I eventually moved into an apartment with two other guys on Blenheim Crescent. I later discovered that we lived next door to the colourful glam rock star Marc Bolan of T. Rex. Blenheim Crescent was just off the famous Portobello Road street market which ran from Notting Hill down into Ladbroke Grove.

The whole area at this time was alive and vibrant. Here was Hippy Ville to the max. On any day you would find the most 'out of this world' people on its streets. Shops sold colourful hippy clothes and accessories, and Hindu and Tibetan prayer flags hung across streets. As you walked around the neighbourhood, especially in the summer, the strains of music, sometimes Indian sitar music or maybe the Grateful Dead or Pink Floyd, would mingle with the smell of fragrant incense which would drift from open windows.

Saturdays, especially, were different, as the whole area filled with people from across London and around the country who came to shop, hang out with friends, or listen to street bands and musicians who would perform under the Ladbroke Grove flyover. This brought two distinct groups together. Those of us who lived in the area considered ourselves hardcore, committed hippies and those who put on their hippy clothes and joined us on Saturdays were what we called weekend hippies. Those of us who were hardcore truly believed we could build an ideal world filled with peace, love and spirituality.

Sadly, as time went on, a third group began to emerge. Drugs were always part of the hippy scene and smoking marijuana and taking LSD were common. Excessive use by some people led to addiction to heroin and other heavy drugs resulting in destroyed lives and, in some instances, death. It was tragic to see people deteriorate physically, mentally and emotionally as the demon of drug addiction gripped their lives. At this point the hippy movement began its decline as people became disillusioned and began to give up on the dream.

Living in the area, I became integrated into the community and became friends with lots of people. Seeing the needs of people coming to Portobello Road to shop for hippy clothes and accessories, I later developed a small business selling things at the Saturday hippy market. It didn't take long to get to know people who I would meet on a day-to-day basis. Like many others at that time, I was searching for something deeper in my life and, like many other young people, turned to New Age spirituality with its mix of Hindu and Buddhist philosophies and ideas.

Spirituality, or religion, had never played a major part in my growing up, as it was never really all that important to us. What was really valued was building one's own life through hard work and discipline. My parents did consider themselves Christians, though, and instilled many Christian values into me as a child, but church never played a major role in our lives except that I went to Sunday school a few times. I always strongly believed in God but saw him as someone who was distant and unreachable. I had never heard that he loved me and that, through Jesus, I could have a personal relationship with him. Looking back now, I can recognise that I had a hunger for God, but having a relationship with him through Jesus was something that was totally alien to me at the time.

London at that time had plenty to offer in terms of New Age spirituality. The Beatles had brought the Maharishi from India to the UK and imported the practice of meditation. Following the Maharishi's footsteps, many other gurus came, setting up various brands of Hinduism and Buddhism that attracted many followers. On any given day in Oxford Street, London's biggest shopping area, you would hear the chant of 'Hare Krishna' sung out to the sound of Indian drums and finger cymbals as saffron-robed devotees danced their way through the crowds. I visited their temple on Bury Road many times and got to know some of the devotees. At one point I spent several weeks living in the temple so that I could learn more of what they believed. A great experience for me at that time was being invited to sing with them on the album they produced at Abbey Road Studios, which was owned by The Beatles and where I got to meet George Harrison – a great, humble guy filled with love and who, in my opinion, was deeply spiritual and searching in his own way.

Living in Notting Hill I became part of the Quintessence Community. This was a small, relational community of people led by Indian guru Swami Ambikananda and was made up of a group of friends who were searching for deeper spiritual meaning in their lives. This was not a community where we actually lived together, as some did in hippy communes operating at that time, but we lived in separate apartments and met regularly. As well as meeting socially, we would gather together to meditate and listen to teachings from the guru.

Central to the community was the music band Quintessence, who had a large following across the nation's hippy community and played in concerts and major music festivals, like Glastonbury and others, across the UK and Europe. One of their songs was about Notting Hill Gate and how great everything looked there and, for me, living in Notting Hill Gate at this time was an exciting place to be. Life was good, and I was living in one of the most exciting places to be in England at the time. Yet there was something major missing in my life. If only I could figure out what it was. My spiritual longing continued.

Around that time people were returning from the hippy trail, which stretched from London to India and, for some, further on to Kathmandu, Nepal. I was becoming increasingly dissatisfied with my life, which created in me a strong desire to find God. Although, like so many others, I had listened to Indian gurus and sought spirituality through Eastern religion, I still had a void within. At that time I developed a deep desire to find God. As people returned from India, they brought with them amazing stories of Indian spirituality and its gods, gurus, ashrams and temples. From the exotic, palm-fringed, sun-drenched beaches of Goa to the lush green valleys of Nepal, there were stories to tell.

Because of my sense of adventure and desire to travel since childhood, all this appealed to me. As I listened to the tales of those who had returned from the overland route to India and Nepal, I was stirred to head out on the famous hippy trail. However, for me, the main reason was to not just travel but to find God. India, with its deep spirituality and religion, was calling me, and I felt that maybe this would be where I would find the God I was looking for.

The hippy trail, as it became known in the sixties and seventies, attracted tens of thousands of young people along its route, creating a whole new generation of world nomads. Most came from Western Europe or North America, and while some were seeking to extend their desire to drop out of Western society, many travelled in search of peace, happiness or enlightenment. A few hitchhiked along the trail, but most travelled by local transport. There were some buses which brought travellers overland from Europe, two of which, I remember, were the Magic Bus and the Chapati Express. No one really had deadlines and people wandered at leisure, staying in each place as long as they desired.

Clusters of budget hotels and restaurants sprung up along the way catering to those who travelled. These became resting places, as well as information centres, where travellers would report on what was happening along the trail. As things were always in a process of change, those returning from India would share the latest news on where to sleep or eat, or where the best places were to obtain visas for the next leg of the journey. With Istanbul being the gateway to the East, the famous Pudding Shop became a major place for this as people posted messages with relevant information on one of its walls. Most people had very little money and travelled light.

In the meantime, my inner search continued, and in slow, visible ways, God was beginning to respond to my longing for him. Often people have many small 'God encounters' on their journey to know him, and this was the case with me. During that time I visited my parents, and while opening a drawer to look for something, I noticed a small red booklet among some papers. Drawn to it, I pulled it out and read the title. It was a printed copy of the Gospel of John, which had been given to my mother during a recent stay in hospital. I opened the pages and began to read. Something inside me was drawing me to the words and message. I was both fascinated and attracted to this man Jesus and his teaching.

Until then I had never read the Bible and had no real understanding of Christianity. I had never heard a full explanation of the good news of the gospel message Jesus came to bring. I had only experienced traditional church on very rare occasions and although I had learned about Jesus I never fully heard, or understood, that I could have a personal relationship with God through him. I felt that church held very little relevance to my life. Hinduism and Buddhism seemed much more colourful and experiential, and for me and many other young people, it held a greater attraction. However, this Jesus I began to read about seemed different, and something stirred within me as I read his words.

Following this, something new was becoming evident in Portobello Road in its famous Saturday market. I began to notice small groups of hippies talking about Jesus. This was surprising, as we had always identified Christianity with the culture we had moved away from. I later learned that what became known as the Jesus movement had broken out on the West Coast of the United States. Thousands of hippies, realising that their lifestyle and beliefs were empty and held nothing for them, were turning to Jesus, where they found new life and an end to their spiritual search. Fuelling this was a discovery of a grass roots Christianity which was led by Jesus, who preached a radical message of love and peace which seemed to go beyond empty religion.

This was something new, refreshing and attractive to so many young people at that time. As people looked beyond

Christianity as a religion, they discovered an experiential relationship and a new life with God through Jesus. Those who aligned themselves to this movement became known as 'Jesus People' or 'Jesus Freaks' and they began to emerge among the London hippy scene. They lived simply, shared what they had with others and proclaimed a positive message of a God of love who longed for a relationship with those he had created.

So here again was this Jesus. Up to this point I didn't know how to have a relationship with him, nor was I convinced that Jesus was the way for me, but something was happening and stirring within me. The date had now been set for me to leave London with two other friends on the hippy trail heading East. We were due to leave in September, stay in India over the winter months and return to England the following year.

As we approached the time to leave, something came up which prevented me from leaving on that specific date. Knowing that there were hundreds of people travelling out to Asia at that time, and that I would make friends with others along the way, I told the other two guys to leave as planned. I would leave about two weeks later than them, they would leave information for me along the way, and I would meet up with them either along the route or in India itself. I believe that this was part of God's plan as he was working behind the scenes of my life in order to draw me to himself.

As I continued my search for God two more significant things happened before I left the UK. The first was a strange encounter with the Indian guru. In the Quintessence community, an evening was planned where individuals would go through an initiation ceremony where the guru would give them a new name and assign them to worship a Hindu god. The name given was usually the name of a prominent Hindu god. This was to be a new beginning or a 'new birth' for the individuals who were invited to the ceremony. I was one of the few people invited to participate, and I eagerly looked forward to it, thinking that maybe this would help me move forward in my spiritual search. It would also enable me to enter more fully into the community I had now become a part of.

The evening arrived, and I climbed the stairs to the Notting Hill apartment where the gathering would take place. The room was slightly darkened, and candles and incense burned on an altar to Hindu gods. The singing began with Hindu worship chants, which began to rise in intensity as some people began to move into prayerful, trance-like states. The place felt charged with spiritual energy. After the singing the guru gave a short discourse until it was time for the initiations to begin. As each individual was called forward, he placed his hands on each one, gave them their new name, and told them the name of the god they were to serve and worship. As each person received from the guru, their faces glowed with a spiritual ecstasy.

Now my time came. I stood before the guru. I felt both nervous and excited and I could feel my heart pounding in my chest. As I looked at him his face suddenly changed. I can't explain how, but it was as if he saw something behind me. As his expression changed, he moved back, slightly away from me. For a moment he seemed unsettled, even afraid. Whatever it was that he had experienced, he could not progress with what he was about to do. I was confused by his action and looked at him, trying to figure out what had just happened. Everyone else in the group looked confused too. Suddenly he looked at me and with a very serious tone to his voice uttered these words, 'You belong to Jesus and must follow him.'

I was taken aback! I went home that evening thinking over what had taken place. I wondered what had happened that had caused him to do something he had probably never done before. Why had he drawn back when I stood before him? What had he seen? Why me? Here was another encounter involving Jesus. As I had been sincerely praying that I would somehow find God, I was being increasingly drawn to Jesus. The guru never explained what had happened to him that evening or what he had seen. In fact, I never actually saw him again, as I left shortly after this for India.

The second thing happened a few weeks later. My friends had left England and headed out on the hippy trail, and I had two more weeks in London before I too would leave and travel East. One midweek afternoon I was walking down Oxford Street. As usual, the road was filled with large black London cabs and double-decker buses. Pavements held crowds of people shopping or taking lunch breaks from the surrounding offices or shops. As I walked past the Salvation Army building, a young man approached me. He had a short beard, long dark hair and wore jeans and a casual shirt. As he approached, he spoke with an American accent.

Usually, I didn't engage with people who would try to stop me on the street, but this time I felt almost arrested on the spot and stopped to talk to him. As I fixed my eyes on his, in order to engage in conversation, I sensed there was something different about him. He began to share with me things I had never heard before. He told me that he felt God had spoken to him about me as he saw me walking towards him. He said that God knew I was searching for him and wanted me to know that he loved me and was reaching out to have a relationship with me. With tears in his eyes, he went on to say that Jesus loved me so much and that he had died for me on the cross in order to bring me into a relationship with God. All I had to do was believe in Jesus, surrender my life to him and accept the wonderful gift that he offered. I was amazed, stunned and confused by these words. Could it be true? Could getting to know God be that easy? I had never heard this before. I thanked him as he placed a piece of literature into my hand. I walked off deeply pondering all of the things he had said as I went. 'Don't forget,' he called after me. 'Jesus loves you.'

I walked away with those words ringing in my ears and burning in my heart. *Jesus loves you.* Three words which have remained with me and have given me strength and guided me through the years. Whatever happens in my life, I trust in God's love. I always know that, somehow, he will work things out for me in the best possible way. I didn't fully understand everything that had been said to me that day and was not sure what to do next. Here was this Jesus again. It began to seem that wherever I turned I would encounter him and be faced with his love for me.

Jesus loves you. The words went over and over in my heart and mind. That evening I read through the booklet he had given me, and at the end I prayed a heartfelt prayer telling God that I didn't understand what was happening to me but that I wanted to know him. I had not surrendered my life to Christ and didn't really know how to do so. I was still unsure, or even unclear, about this 'Jesus thing' but my heart was wide open to whatever I had to do next.

I found out later that, through this whole time, a Christian lady who lived in the community where I had grown up was praying for me. She didn't really know me, but God had placed me on her heart, and she began praying that I would come to faith in Christ. Without knowing where I was or what was going on in my life, she continued to pray, believing that God was leading her and that he would work in my life.

I thank God that behind the scenes he was at work in the circumstances of my life in a way that would bring me to a place where I would come to know him. I was about to discover that this would happen in a very unusual way.

3

On the Hippy Trail

It was 1972 and I had spent around three years in London. As I stood by the roadside at the edge of the city, a white van pulled up with two guys inside.

'Where are you headed?' one of them asked.

'Dover,' I replied.

The port of Dover, famous for its white cliffs, is a departure point for ferries crossing the English Channel to Calais, France. I climbed into the vehicle, thankful for the warmth, and we chatted as we headed for Dover.

Arriving at the ferry terminal, I met another group of young people who were heading out East. We boarded the ferry and arrived in France in the early hours of the morning. As I walked away from the terminal, the port area was starting to come alive as people began their preparations for the day. Small French cafés spilled out tables and chairs onto pavements and breakfasts were being prepared. I was so excited, as this was my first time out of the UK and it felt good to be on foreign soil.

My journey had begun, and I was excited about what I would discover and experience in distant lands. My plan was still to hitchhike across Europe, and I thought I would stand a better chance of hitching if I travelled alone rather than with others I had met on the ferry. This worked well for me, and I was able to get lifts across Belgium and into Germany arriving on the outskirts of Cologne late that evening.

I joined several others who were standing by the road that led onto the autobahn, each one hoping for a lift. It felt like I had been there for hours. Time dragged on as I stood in the cold and the rain which, whipped by a biting wind, seemed to penetrate right through to my bones. Car after car drove by, and raindrop after cold raindrop pounded my body as I stood by the side of the road. You can imagine that I now began to rethink this idea about hitchhiking across Europe. After some time, I decided to change my plans.

Making my way into Cologne I walked up to the counter at the train station and purchased a ticket which would take me to Munich and from there to Istanbul, Turkey. This took a large amount out of my budget, but once I was in the comfort of the warm train and was able to dry out the wet clothes I was wearing, I knew I had made the right decision. This was no luxurious *Orient Express*, but it was certainly better than the hitchhiking idea.

I took my seat on the train leaving Munich and looked at the young guy sitting opposite. I asked him where he was headed. Pleasantly surprised, I was happy to hear him respond in English. He was from the US and was travelling to India. I was pleased to strike up a friendship with him, and it felt good to know that we would at least travel on some of the journey together, which we did. He was planning to spend several months living in a Hindu community in his own search for God.

The trip across Europe was amazing. We wound our way through the German countryside and crossed the border into Austria, where small towns and picturesque villages nestled against awesome mountains. Continuing on, we travelled across what was then Yugoslavia, and then Bulgaria. As interesting as these countries were, my main focus was Istanbul, the gateway to the East, from where I would begin to encounter distant lands shrouded in mystery and adventure.

As we crossed the border into Turkey, the terrain became increasingly dry and more barren with a beauty all of its own. Small farmhouses appeared across the landscape and shepherds grazed their flocks across the open spaces. As we approached Istanbul, the atmosphere in the train began to fill with excitement as people busied themselves in preparation for our arrival. Where our journey had been more sedate due to constant travel, there was now loud chatter and hustle and bustle as people started to gather up their belongings. Suitcases, bags and bundles were placed here and there as, after long periods of separation, Turkish people who were now settled into new lives in Europe were getting ready to be reunited with family and friends.

We were now edging the Sea of Marmara as we entered the outskirts of the great city of Istanbul. We travelled past houses tightly packed together, some of which had been built many years previously and each adorned with intricate, wood-carved windows and balconies. I wondered what stories each one would have to tell of generations of families who had lived within their walls. Now we passed streets filled with people until we entered the great train station where, with the sound of the horn and the screech and clatter of metal wheels upon the tracks, we came to a halt at this present part of our journey: Istanbul.

I found Istanbul to be an amazingly vibrant city with a colourful history, which could be seen in its ancient mosques and buildings. It is the largest city in Turkey, and had once been a centre of learning and power known far and wide for its wealth and beauty. It has been occupied by the Greeks and Romans, followed by the Ottoman Empire, and has survived to become the city it is today.

Istanbul was everything I imagined it to be and looked every bit like a city of the East. We made our way through narrow, winding streets which were filled with people. The gentle autumn sun caressed the city and the chatter of buying and selling mingled with the aroma of delicately spiced food. While young men carried loads of merchandise upon their strong backs, old men sat at roadside cafés drinking tea and watching the world move slowly on.

We came to our hotel, which was situated opposite the famed Sultan Ahmed Mosque, also known as the Blue Mosque. The Sultanahmet area was the place to find budget hotels and hostels and was the gathering point for travellers moving either further east or returning from India or Nepal. It was also the place to meet people on their way back from the East, where one could gather the latest information gleaned from travelling along the hippy trail.

I spent a week in this incredible city and discovered that within its skyline of domes and minarets it still contained reflections of its glorious past. Each morning I would wake to the melodious voice of the muezzin as he called the faithful to prayer. After breakfast I would spend the day exploring the city. I walked the narrow streets and alleyways talking with people and wandering through a maze of bazaars which were filled with glittering objects of colour and beauty. I would discover a simple Turkish eatery hidden away somewhere and enjoy lunch. In the heat of the afternoon, I would sit on the rich carpets of the Blue Mosque where I would enjoy the cool, gentle breeze that slowly travelled through its chambers. Its architectural grandeur and beauty were awe-inspiring.

Then, in the evening, I would head for Istanbul's famous Pudding Shop where I would mingle with other travellers and gather information they had obtained along the road. I'd also check out the wall, which was covered with notes left by travellers giving information relating to the hippy trail or advertising empty seats in cars or buses heading East or West. And of course, I always enjoyed the famous rice pudding, from where the café got its name. My whole time there conjured up within me everything I had felt or imagined about the East, and Istanbul brought afresh to my imagination stories I'd read as a child.

I would have loved to have spent more time in this delightful city, but I knew, after almost one week, that it was now time to move on. I was about to make the journey of a lifetime along what was once part of the ancient and mysterious Silk Road. I would follow in the footsteps of Alexander the Great, Marco Polo, Persians and traders who had trekked along these well-established caravan routes along hot, dusty deserts.

As I left the streets of this gateway city to the lands of the East, what would I find? Would my expectations be met or would I be disappointed? Would everything be smooth sailing or would I encounter danger? What new experiences would await me? Added to that was the fact that I only had enough money to get to India, and beyond that I had no plan. I knew that if I was to turn back, this was the place to do it as I still had enough money to return to the UK. Going forward was a great risk, and I seriously considered if my next step would really work out. Should I move safely back through Europe to England, or forward into the unknown? With thousands of miles ahead of me along one of the world's most ancient routes, and not knowing what would await me as I stepped out into the unknown, I made my decision. I would go forward.

I prepared to cross the Bosporus strait, a stretch of water connecting the Black Sea in the north to the Sea of Marmara in the south, thus creating a geographical boundary dividing

Istanbul between Europe and Asia. Ferries, tankers and fishing boats ploughed through its deep waters. All around me was the hustle and bustle of people along the water's edge and the shouts of street food sellers mingled with the various aromas of their delicious food. Added to the human voices was the sound of seagulls, their shrill call filling the air as they swooped towards the ground in search of scraps of discarded food.

I crossed the Bosporus by ferry and, saying goodbye to the West and looking to the East, I headed for the train station on the Asian side. I purchased my ticket and boarded a train headed for Erzurum, a city near the Iranian border, and the next leg of my journey had begun.

The two days' train journey covered central Turkey and was awesome. At times we travelled past fertile fields which would change to arid desert, then we would make our way through mountain passes. The train made its way through small towns and villages, some of which were quite remote, and because of this, much of life went on as it had done for centuries. As shepherds tended their sheep across grasslands, other people were busy working in the fields. As we headed east, the dress and architecture began to change until we arrived in eastern Turkey, which had more of a Middle Eastern feel. We passed Mount Ararat, the sacred mountain which some believe still holds the ark of Noah, and arrived in Erzurum, the city of Kurds, from where we would head for the Iranian border.

Crossing the border into Iran, I headed for the city of Tabriz. Iran was immediately different from Turkey. Women here were more veiled by wearing the *chador*, and the landscape became more arid. From Tabriz, I travelled on to the capital city of Tehran, which was more modern and much more developed than most of the rest of the country. Arriving in the city I checked into a hotel which had been recommended by other travellers and, after spending a few days wandering the streets and bazaars of Tehran, I headed towards the city of Meshad, located near the eastern border where Iran meets Afghanistan. Meshad is one of Iran's holy cities and a pilgrimage site for devout Muslims.

Once again, travelling across Iran was an incredible experience, and I feel privileged to have been able to visit this country when it was possible to travel so freely across this land. What allowed the freedom to travel at that time was that Iran was still ruled by Mohammad Reza Pahlavi, the Shah of Iran. In an effort to modernise the country, the Shah brought about measures to increase the economy, modernise the military, give women greater freedom and turn Iran into a global power. Iran became oil rich. Many foreigners lived there at that time and there was greater freedom to travel. This continued until the exiled Ruhollah Khomeini (Ayatollah Khomeini) returned and established the Islamic Republic of Iran, which ended centuries of monarchy. From that time Iran, like Afghanistan, become pretty much closed to outside travellers.

I actually regret not spending more time in Iran when there was so much freedom to travel, but who could know what the future would hold? I grew to love the place and the people. I didn't know it at the time, but several years later I would have an amazing time leading a church made up of Iranians, but that's a story for later. I do feel privileged, though, to have been able to travel at a time before everything began to change, not always for the better. I was able to see a world that was at the end of an era. International tourism, modernisation and access to Western culture through satellite TV and the internet brought about an influence that would bring drastic change to some of these nations, while hard-line Islam in Iran and war in Afghanistan caused their borders to close to the outside world.

Thankfully, I got to travel through these nations before these changes took place, where I could experience the world as it used to be.

I crossed the border and entered the enchanting and incredible nation of Afghanistan. I actually planned to travel through Afghanistan, just spending a short time there, as my goal was to get to India. I didn't know it at the time, but God had other plans, and something was about to happen which would keep me in that ancient land longer than anticipated. My life was about to be disrupted, and changed, in a very dramatic way.

4

Afghanistan

As we crossed the border and entered Afghanistan, we travelled through the border town of Islam Qala and crossed a barren wilderness until we came to the ancient city of Herat. City names like Herat, Kandahar and Kabul are all places we are familiar with today, but when I travelled in 1972, I suspect most people hadn't even heard of Afghanistan. As our rickety old bus approached this great oasis city of the desert, the sun was setting in the Eastern sky. We made our way along narrow streets lined with mud-brick houses. As the first shadows of night engulfed the city, a gentle glow of light, from oil lamps, spilled out into the darkness from doors and windows. I arrived at our hotel, and after a shower and a light meal, drifted into a deep sleep.

I woke early the next morning eager to explore this ancient city, which is rich in history and culture. Although it has a written history dating back many years, no one is exactly sure of its beginnings. A key city on the ancient silk route, Herat was connected with the Mediterranean to the west, and China and India to the east. I was able to explore the many ancient ruins, which include a majestic fort built by Alexander the Great, as well as the city's exquisitely decorated minarets.

I discovered that Herat had been a battleground of many of the world's greatest conquering armies, who shed blood upon its soil and ruled over its people. The Arabs made it the centre of the Muslim world and Timur the Turk developed it into a centre of intellect, art, science and culture and made it famous for carpets, textiles and miniature paintings. It was interesting to see such a wide mix of ethnic groups across the city. The more oriental-looking Tajiks, Hazaras, Uzbeks and Turkmen mingled with Pashtuns, and along the edges of the city were the encampments of the Persian-speaking Kuchi nomads.

Our hotel was situated on a large, main street. Although it was a major thoroughfare, it still remained a dirt road covered with a thick layer of dust, which blew up in clouds as *tongas*, the horse-drawn carriages used as taxis, moved hurriedly along. I walked through sun-drenched streets which were alive with the colour and the hustle and bustle of Eastern life. Wandering down back alleys, I came into a maze of small streets which were made up of bazaars where you could buy anything you needed. Overflowing out onto the streets from open-fronted shops were beautiful Afghan carpets with rich designs dating back for centuries, and coloured red from dyes extracted from the juice of pomegranates.

In the next section, shops were filled with brightly coloured fabrics carried in from Pakistan, Iran, China and Russia. Next there were the sellers of fruit and nuts with their great mountains of walnuts, almonds and pistachios alongside pomegranates, apples, oranges, dates, figs and great mounds of watermelons in abundance. I practically lived on all of these every day.

I would then catch the aroma of warm, freshly baked whole wheat *naan* and kebabs roasting on the open fires, which would encourage me to eat. There were so many eateries where someone would call out, giving an invitation to those passing by. All across Afghanistan these small, family run restaurants would spill out onto the streets where most of the cooking was done, barbecue-style, on open charcoal fires. Most of what was on offer were lamb kebabs. Succulent pieces of lamb were placed onto skewers and roasted over burning coals by the 'gourmet chef'. Standing over the coals with fan in hand, he would wave the fan back and forth at a frenzied speed until the meat was cooked and the kebabs were ready. This would be eaten with freshly baked *naan* and washed down with large quantities of hot sweet tea, drunk from a glass. I was fascinated by the teapots the tea was poured from. The standard favourites were teapots from China, which were very often cracked and pieced back together with glue and wire which somehow held it all in one piece.

Being a strong Muslim nation, very few women were to be seen on the streets. Those who did venture outdoors were always covered with a *burqa*, the traditional outer covering worn by women in Afghanistan. The *burqa* in Afghanistan is different from forms of coverings used in other Muslim nations. It consists of a large piece of fine fabric which covers the whole body from head to foot. Beginning with what looks like a small, delicately embroidered cap which fits onto the head, the rest of the fabric, which is attached to the headpiece, falls to the feet. The opening across the face is covered with woven thread which forms a kind of lattice work. This enables the wearer to look out but no one to see the face. These women would appear like ethereal spirits floating in the clouds of dust rising from the passing *tongas*, and I often wondered how they could actually see where they were going. I was told that an Afghan man learns to tell a woman's age by her ankles.

While the women were covered and restricted, the men lived in greater freedom. Their clothes consisted of a loose shirt worn outside their trousers and which came down to the knees. The front of the shirt would be embroidered with fine threads showing intricate, artistic needlework, often with small glass beads woven into the threads. Their trousers were made up of large amounts of fabric, baggy, gathered at the waist and narrowing at the bottoms. They also wore sturdy black leather sandals and, of course – to add some drama to the outfit – a turban, which was made up of a great length of material wrapped several times around the head, giving a Lawrence of Arabia effect. Black *kajal*, or *kohl*, would often be worn around the eyes.

This was definitely a man's world where women were covered and kept, for most of the time, behind closed doors. Because of this, my only social contact with others was to communicate with men, which was easy as every Afghan I encountered was very warm, hospitable and eager to talk, especially to practise English. The other thing I noticed was the sense of macho bravado the men carried. The Afghan men are magnificent horse riders and their favourite sport is *buzkashi*, a wild, fast and aggressive game carried out on horseback. This game is similar to polo but uses the carcass of a dead goat, which is caught and dragged by hand, instead of a ball, and is definitely played more aggressively.

I saw further evidence of aggression one evening when I heard frenzied shouting on the street below my hotel window. As this caught my attention, I opened the doors leading to the balcony from where I could clearly see what was happening. Below me was a crowd of around twenty men moving with excited shouts and gestures. A fight had broken out, and in the centre of the crowd were two men who were alive with quick, sharp movements. Arms and legs were moving speedily as each sought to dodge the other's blow. Then, in the dim light which shone out into the shadows, I noticed one of the men pull a knife from within his waistcoat. Now the mob cheered with even more excitement as they disappeared down a side street.

I found Herat, like all of Afghanistan, to be a beautiful, wild, rugged and enchanting place. If Istanbul had reminded me of the stories I'd read as a child of exotic places, then being in Herat was like falling into the pages and becoming one of the characters. My one-week stay seemed too short, but it was time to move on.

With bags and bundles piled on top of the old bus I climbed inside and, taking my seat among Afghans and a handful of hippy travellers, we made our way out of the city. Now we were on the road that crossed the Afghan desert towards the city of Kandahar where, after an overnight stop, we would journey on to Kabul. For two days we travelled across this mysterious land. Stretching out in every direction was a dry, barren desert, an ocean without water. For many hours our dust-covered bus moved slowly along the road, which was built across miles of wilderness. Even though we kept the windows of the bus closed, tiny particles of dust would find their way inside until we were covered with these powdery particles of the desert. In fact, as I write this and just think about it, I can still almost feel the dust and take in the smell of its dryness.

Journeying on, the bus lazily made its way across the arid landscape. To the north, the barren terrain stretched out until it rose into majestic mountains. If my goal had not been India, I would have loved to have headed out to explore the mountains and experience what lay within their valleys. On every other side, as far as the eye could see, the desert rolled out, only being interrupted by mud-walled villages some distance from the road. These appeared out of nowhere. They looked as if they had been raised up and built from the very earth on which they stood, giving the appearance of sandcastles upon a long, lonely beach.

Every once in a while, the beige barrenness of the landscape was broken by groups of Kuchi nomads, the people of
Afghanistan who fascinated me the most. These nomads of the
desert would arise out of nowhere, like the sun rising at dawn.
Picture a long caravan of camels, donkeys, people and sheep
moving in unhurried slow motion across the desert with a sense
of serene calm. Having no contact with, or little knowledge of,
the outside world, the desert for these people is the only world
they know.

Like a splash of colour painted on a canvas of gold, they were
like the work of a master artist, created with brushes dipped
in paint of vivid colour and life. No man-made border con-
fined them, and they belonged to no one. Going wherever the
seasons took them, they were as free as the wind. If our bus
approached them on the road, they would erupt with noise,
shouting and an outbreak of activity as camels, sheep and donkeys scattered at the sound of the vehicle's approach. Then all
would return to its original order as this ancient scene made its
way along centuries-old paths.

Among the Kuchis, the men dressed in traditional Afghan
clothes except for the deep red velvet waistcoats that were
embroidered in exquisite patterns with thick, gold-coloured
thread. The women, however, were different from the other
women of Afghanistan. Unlike the women of the cities, towns
and villages, there were no covered faces here. Instead, they
wore a large piece of colourful material which covered the
head and shoulders but not the face. Their colourful, flowing
dresses, which came below the knee, were made of fabric intricately embroidered across the front with fine threads sewn
into patterns which had been handed down from generation
to generation. Small pieces of mirror would be worked into
the threads. Their trousers were again made of great lengths

of coloured fabric which, like those worn by the men, were gathered at the ankles. Their shoes, when worn, were made of rugged leather embroidered with gold coloured threads. Ears, neck, wrists and ankles would be adorned with the silver jewellery of the desert tribes, creating a soft tinkling sound as they moved gracefully. It was interesting to recognise similar jewellery among the nomadic Banjara people of India, which I saw when I visited at a later date.

A thread of culture seemed to connect these nomadic people all the way from the Middle East to India. The sun would set beyond the desert, flooding the eternal sky with brilliant hues. This would provide a magnificent backdrop for the Kuchi encampments. The stage was now set and the scenery in place as clusters of black Bedouin tents, set around campfires, were silhouetted against the fading light. Standing as a monument in time, and unchanged by the madness of a fast-changing world, this could have been Abraham and his people centuries before.

Leaving the barren landscape of the desert, the bus began to approach Afghanistan's capital city, Kabul. Walled houses began to increase in number, and we drove through streets occupied with increasing numbers of people. After two days of open, uninhabited spaces it felt strange to be back in urban landscape again. As we headed into Kabul, the sun was beginning to set across the Eastern sky, casting a hue of pink and gold upon the mountains raised above the city. The bus pulled into what I suspected was the city's main bus station: an open area of dirt ground. Our vehicle joined other ancient-looking buses waiting to head for their next destination, and we came to the end of this part of our journey.

I checked into a hotel on the famous Chicken Street. This street was an area well known along the hippy trail as the place to stay while in Kabul. Running along both sides of the street was an array of shops selling Afghan carpets, antiques, jewellery and clothes. A few other grocery shops, as well as a bakery, stocked a few Western items. The rest of the street was made up of budget hotels and restaurants catering to travellers passing through Kabul in one direction or the other. And, of course, there were the chickens which gave the street its name.

Not only was it inhabited by these feathery creatures, but it was also filled with some of the most weird and wonderful people ever known. By now, those who were travelling east from Europe had exchanged their Western clothes for the more exotic hippy fashion available on Chicken Street, and those returning from India wore equally exotic garments from that part of the world. This was definitely a major place to stay for a good few days to soak up the atmosphere and listen to the stories. Restaurants and *chai* shops were the main places to hang out, eat good food and drink *chai* (tea). Every evening travellers would gather together and, sitting on cushions on the floor around low tables, we would listen to tales of the road to the sounds of Cat Stevens, Jimi Hendrix, the Cream, or some other sounds of the hippy sixties.

Here were the veterans of the East, the gurus of the road who knew where to travel, and where to sleep or eat along the trail. These were the people who had lived on the beaches of Goa or in the hills surrounding Kathmandu or Manali for a long period of time and were now heading back to Europe or America. Usually, they had run out of money and were heading back so they could work and save up enough to return.

Living in that part of the world was cheap then, and you could live on very little for a very long time. With their sun-kissed skin, exotic clothing and tribal jewellery collected from near and far, we looked up to these people almost as if they were saints. We also looked forward to the day when we would return and receive the same respect and admiration. After all, 'doing India', as we used to say in those days, was the ultimate achievement which moved you up the hippy culture ladder. Each one brought back enchanting and exciting stories from India and Nepal. All of this continued to whet my appetite to move on. However, although I was only planning to stay in Kabul for a short time, something was about to happen which would hold me in the city for a longer period than I anticipated.

At the hotel where I was staying, I met three German guys who were sharing a large room which contained four beds. As I got to know them, I realised that by moving in with them I could save a lot of money on my hotel bill, so I moved into their room. After a couple of days, I woke up one morning severely ill. The other guys had left the room and I was alone. As I lay on the bed, I felt extremely weak and nauseous. The air was warm and dry from the heat and dust-filled atmosphere. My sinuses and throat felt raw and dried out. When I moved, the room seemed to be spinning, and I longed for some water and cool air. Suddenly, a feeling of intense nausea rose up inside and I knew I needed to quickly head for the bathroom where I would be sick. The shared bathroom was situated in the hallway outside our room.

I pulled myself up, holding the side of the bed, and slid my feet into my leather sandals, which were on the grey cement floor beneath me. Then, barely able to stand and feeling weak and dizzy, I staggered towards the door. Just as I was about to open it, I remembered that I had left my travel wallet, which contained my passport and all of my money, under my pillow where I had been sleeping. I turned to take it, not wanting to leave it in the room while I was gone. Sliding my hand under the pillow, I located the cloth wallet which I carried under my clothes when I travelled. In those days there were no ATM cashpoints, and obtaining money from home through banks was possible but could take weeks, and sometimes it didn't arrive at all. For those reasons we carried all of the money we needed for our travels on our person. Picking up the wallet, I held it in my hand and headed for the bathroom.

Going into the bathroom, I placed the wallet on the windowsill and was violently sick. Still feeling overcome with weakness I returned to my room and collapsed onto the bed. I took deep breaths and willed myself to get better. The room was still and quiet as I lay there for several more minutes, staring at the white ceiling. Then it hit me. I had left my wallet, which contained my passport and all my money, in the bathroom.

The realisation of what I had done suddenly struck me with a wave of panic. All the money I possessed was in that wallet. Gripped by fear, and visualising all my money gone, I immediately had thoughts of the worst possible scenarios. What would happen if the money was stolen? How would I pay my bills? Would I be stranded in Kabul? How would I buy food? Would the hotel let me stay? What would I do and where could I turn? I knew that leaving anything valuable anywhere unattended, even for a few seconds, would stand a good chance of being stolen. At 19 years old and on my own in a strange, alien country without family or friends, I found this very scary. I hoped and prayed that my money was still there.

Through sheer willpower I drew on what strength I had and, once again, made my way to the bathroom, praying all the time that my money would be there. I felt even more sick as I moved across the hall. The heat and the dry air moving in from the desert was stifling. Placing my hand on the handle of the bathroom door, my heart was beating and my mouth was dry as I pushed the door open. It was unlocked and this was a good sign. There was no one inside, so maybe no one had been in there after all.

I entered the bathroom and silently prayed. 'Oh God, please, please let it be there.' I immediately looked to the place where I had left my wallet, and with a sigh of utter, joyful relief, I saw that it was exactly where I'd left it. I felt the pressure and feeling of fear diminish. I was so thankful and relieved that it was still there and realised how stupid I had been to panic. After all, I'd only been gone for a few minutes. I walked across the room smiling to myself and feeling grateful for being spared what could have been a horrendous outcome. I reached up towards the windowsill, and placing my fingers around the wallet, I took it in my hand. It felt different. All my money was gone.

5

Finding Christ in Kabul

'I'd like to report some stolen travellers' cheques.' I looked at the guy behind the counter at the American Express office. I was thankful that, before I had left England, I had converted my cash into travellers' cheques, which every traveller used at that time. If they were stolen, they could be replaced, although this could take a little time and effort, especially in somewhere like Afghanistan.

'Fill out this form.' He handed me a sheet of paper and looked like he had done this many times before.

'How long will it take before they are refunded?'

'Several weeks, maybe more.'

'Several weeks!' My heart sank, as I had thought travellers' cheques would be replaced quicker than that. 'But what do I do in the meantime?'

'I'm sorry, there's nothing more we can do. You'll just have to wait.'

I left the office wondering what my next step should be. The manager at my hotel said I could stay there and settle the bill when my money came through, for which I was very, very grateful. I still needed to eat and had some Afghan money, which had been in my jeans pocket, but this would only last a few days. After that I didn't know what I would do. Fortunately, whoever stole my money had left my passport, something I didn't understand as passports were very valuable when sold on the black market. The other thing that concerned me was that I was losing valuable time by staying in Kabul when I really wanted to move on to India. I just had to get some help from somewhere. I thought over the situation and wondered what I could do. If only I could find some short-term help.

I knew that in foreign countries, if someone was travelling and found themselves in any kind of trouble, they could contact their embassy for help. I also knew that what I was going through probably wouldn't come under the category of a major emergency in their eyes, but I decided to give it a try. I located the address of the British Embassy and headed out on foot across the city streets where I took smaller back roads and asked for directions along the way.

At one point a young Afghan boy was passing by. As he cycled past, I called out asking directions for the embassy. In broken English he indicated that it was not far and, inviting me to sit on the back of his bicycle, offered to take me there. After walking in the scorching sun along hot and dusty roads, I was happy for the lift. By now the streets and houses had become sparser than in the centre of the city. I positioned myself on the metal luggage rack situated above the back wheel of the bicycle and off we went. The dirt roads we travelled along were broken and bumpy in places, and I thought of how a little padding on the seat would have been a wonderful, welcome luxury.

Travelling a short distance, we turned a corner and there before me was the large, white, imposing building of the British Embassy, which stood in a large compound before a backdrop of nearby hills and mountains. This grand, colonial building stood like a great bastion of Britain with the Union Jack flag fluttering in the desert wind. I could understand why it had

been said that it was one of the city's most magnificent buildings. Commissioned in 1919 by Lord Curzon, who had held
a previous position as Viceroy of India, it was intended to be
the finest embassy in Asia. It was very regal. The main building
itself was set in large, open gardens with plants and flower beds
dotted around perfectly manicured lawns. Being surrounded by
dry, barren terrain it stood out like an enormous desert flower.

It was a little bit of Britain in the desert and, in its day,
received visitors from far and wide. Ambassadors, statesmen,
prime ministers, presidents, rajas and shahs would meet within
its corridors to make political decisions, and the very best of
Kabul's high society would attend extravagant parties, which
were held in the spacious ballroom. I pictured them all arriving
dressed in their expensive, perfectly pressed finery and emerging from expensive chauffer-driven vehicles. I arrived covered
in dust on the back of a rickety bicycle pedalled by a boy. Quite
a contrast.

After showing my British passport, I was escorted into the
large, imposing building where I was ushered into a side room.
As I entered, I immediately noticed the Queen looking down
at me from the inner confines of a large wooden frame hanging
from a nail on the wall. I almost felt that I needed to offer an
apology for the mess I'd got myself into. I could practically hear
her say, 'Come along, young man. You are a Britisher abroad
and one must not let down the side. Sort yourself out.'

A young Afghan man sat behind a large desk and asked how
he could help. As I explained what had happened, I got the
impression that he had been here before with many others who
had needed help of one kind or another. He was very compas-
sionate and I could sense his empathy towards both me and
the situation I had found myself in. He went on to explain that
the only way they could help was to arrange a flight back to the

UK. When I returned home, the government would keep my passport until I had paid back the money they had advanced.

I decided that I did not want to give up on my plans but wanted to find a way to go forward. I had come this far and was determined to somehow get the rest of the way. He told me to think about it and come back to see him if I decided I wanted to take that option. I thanked him and rose to leave. As I stood, he reached into his pocket and taking out some cash, handed me some notes. 'Please take this,' he said, 'and if you want you can return it when your money comes through.' I was so touched by this gesture and thanked him. I found the Afghan people to be very warm and hospitable. I made the decision to stay in Kabul, figure out a way forward and not give up on my dream. Making that decision was one of the best I have ever made because things were about to change for me in a powerful way.

I returned to my hotel room as the sun was beginning to set across the city, casting its pink and purple hues across the tops of the surrounding mountains. I slept that night and awoke the next morning and, after taking a shower, went out to find something to eat for breakfast. Later that morning I returned to my room. The other guys were out so I was alone. It was now the end of October and, although the late evenings were much cooler, I could feel the morning daytime heat begin to slowly build. It would be winter soon and the cold weather would set in until spring. The room felt warm and dry.

As I lay down on the bed, I was engulfed with a strange sensation which is difficult to put into words. It seemed that the very atmosphere of the room began to change. Lying in the silence I began to think about my life up to that time. Images began to flash before my eyes as if on a movie screen. This wasn't really a vision, but thoughts and pictures were presented before me. As I looked over my past, all I could see was emptiness and, as I engaged with my present life now, in this silent room, I sensed a deep hunger for God. All I could think about was that, more than anything else in this world, I wanted to know him.

An intense longing rose up inside of me and I began to pray. Tears ran down my face. 'God,' I cried. 'I long for you but cannot find you. I have searched for meaning and purpose in this life. I have looked for answers to my deepest needs. I have sought for you for so long but you cannot be found.' Then, as I waited, in the stillness of the moment words came to me. Not audible words, but words which quietly and tenderly spoke directly to my heart. 'You have searched into many things but you have not sought me. You have not called on my name. I am the answer. I am the truth.' That's all. Just a few words. They reminded me of words I had read earlier in the Gospel of John where Jesus had said he was 'the way and the truth and the life' (John 14:6).

As the room filled with a peaceful presence, I knew deep down inside that this was the voice of Jesus. I realised I had indeed looked in many different directions but had never searched after him or considered following him. Now all of the past encounters I had had, where he was mentioned, began to make sense. Like pieces of a jigsaw puzzle, things were beginning to fall into place. 'Jesus,' I prayed in a very unreligious way. 'I don't know what to do next, but if you can reveal yourself to me more fully and show me what to do, I will follow you.'

On that same day, a short time after this experience, the three German guys I was sharing the room with returned. One of them looked at me. 'Hey, we just met some young American people who live here in Kabul, and they invited us to go to their place for dinner on Thursday evening. Do you want to come?'

Well, anywhere sounded good at this point in time, especially if it involved a free meal. 'We'd better warn you, though,' he went on to say. 'They are Jesus people and they might try to convert us.' He started laughing and I smiled. 'OK,' I thought. 'This sounds strange. Jesus people in Afghanistan. What's going on?' Something leaped inside of me and I somehow sensed this was a major part of what was going on in my life right now. 'This is not just a coincidence,' I thought. 'Maybe God really is at work here after all.' Jesus again.

Thursday evening came and I got ready to head out to where these people lived. I actually felt excited about meeting these Jesus followers, as by now I sensed that all that had been happening to me was a part of some great cosmic plan where God was drawing me to himself. We arrived at the house, where we were welcomed with a warmth that immediately made me feel at ease. The house was reasonably large and stood in a compound. I guessed there were close to around twenty to thirty young people living there. Some were European but mostly North American. None of them looked 'religious' as they all had the long hair and clothes which identified them with the hippy culture. The house was called Dilaram House – Dilaram being a Farsi (Persian) word meaning 'peaceful heart'. Therefore, this was the 'House of the Peaceful Heart'. It certainly felt peaceful.

I was interested to know what had brought these people to Afghanistan and to discover more about the history of the Dilaram community. I learned that it came into being through Floyd and Sally McClung, an American couple, who had come to Kabul to reach out and offer help to people on the hippy trail. At that time, Floyd and Sally were part of a team of young people in India with the Christian organisation Youth With A Mission (YWAM). One day Floyd was approached by an unkempt and emaciated beggar. His first reaction was that this was another Indian beggar among the many others who were on the streets. However, as he looked closer, he realised that this was a young American guy, one of the many travellers who had headed out on the hippy trail. This impacted Floyd deeply. When he returned to America he continued to be haunted by this young man's face and sensed God was asking him to do something to help these people.

This led Floyd to return to Asia, and while in Kabul, he was touched by the needs of hippy travellers in that city. Something was stirring within him as he looked more deeply into the dark side of Kabul's hippy scene. While most people who passed through were untouched by the dark side, many got caught in a destructive web of drug addiction fuelled by readily available cheap heroin. As countries like Turkey and Morocco introduced stringent drug laws, Kabul became the central place for drugs because of its lax regulations. Added to this was the constant dysentery and hepatitis that physically wiped out so many people along the trail.

Some of the travellers, which I'd observed myself, were literally dying through drug addiction and illness. In fact, there was a section of a graveyard that was reserved for hippy travellers who had died from a heroin overdose or other causes. It was common to see people sitting in dark corners of cheap, dilapidated hotels staring vacantly into space. Some would steal or beg on the streets for drug money and would eat leftover food in restaurants. Most of them had sold their passports, which meant they could not leave Kabul and neither could they be identified when they were found dead. Parents in Europe and America would never hear from their children again and would never know how their lives had ended.

It was into this situation that Floyd and Sally arrived. When I met them, I thought they were the most unlikely couple to be called to work with hippy travellers. Both were from strait-laced, evangelical Christian America. They had grown up in Christian families who attended conservative Christian churches, and knew very little of the world they were about to enter. It was obvious that they had a love for those they were reaching out to, and this love enabled them to break all cultural barriers and be accepted into the world of hippies.

Another thing that was happening in Kabul at that time centred around a group of expats working in the city. While living there, they saw the desperate plight of these many young people and felt that something should be done. One key person in this was Christy Wilson, an American pastor, who was leading Afghanistan's only church community. When he met Floyd, he asked him to consider staying in Kabul and setting up a ministry which would help to love, nurture and care for these people. And Dilaram House was born.

I spent my time chatting with people over food until the evening came to a close. Just as I was about to leave, one of the people from the house invited me to visit them the next day. I actually felt a strong connection with the people there, and because of that I decided to return. Friday arrived and I headed out again to Dilaram House and, once again, was warmly welcomed. Deep down inside, something kept telling me that these people had what I was searching for. Added to that was my recent experience in the hotel room where I had prayed to Jesus for direction. Everything in me was drawing me towards Jesus. I knew this was all a part of God's plan but didn't know what steps to take next.

As I got to know those living in the Dilaram community, I discovered three groups of people. Some were Christians who had come to Afghanistan to help Floyd and Sally with what God had called them to do, others were hippy travellers who had become Christians through the ministry of Dilaram, and the third group were those who had been invited to live in the house where they could discover more about Christ and the Christian life.

Influenced by the Jesus movement, this was an open, non-judgemental community of people who sought to live out the Christian life, which was outlined in a very simple way through the teachings of Jesus, whom they had decided to follow. They allowed people to come and live among them, without pressure to become Christians, and would give unconditional help to those who needed it. It was a Christianity I'd never seen before, and the love they had for Jesus, one another and those outside their community appealed to me. When talking to one of the girls, I asked her what had made her decide to come to Afghanistan. I knew that back home in America she could have a very comfortable life and wondered why she would choose to come to Kabul. Her answer surprised me. 'Well,' she said. 'God spoke to me and told me to come.'

God spoke to me! I wondered how God could speak to someone in such a casual way. I knew that I had just had an experience where I sensed words coming to me which I identified as the words of Jesus, but she spoke as if she had a real, personal, permanent relationship with God. I then discovered that the others talked about God in a way which indicated that they knew him. It was almost as if he was a personal friend. This blew me away.

To me, God had always been someone who was distant and not easy to reach or contact. Also, as a child, although I had always believed in God, I'd had the impression that he was a mean, strict, judgemental disciplinarian ready to punish any wrongdoing. Now, through these new friends, I was getting the picture of a loving, gracious God who longed to be in a relationship with the people he had created. Up to that point no one had really explained to me how I could take the important step of getting to know the God they followed, but I was hungry for more. Everything inside me screamed out: *This is your answer. This is it.* I returned to the hotel that evening with much to think about and with an invitation to attend church that Sunday. I was so excited that I could barely wait for Sunday to come.

Sunday morning arrived, and I got into a taxi with some of the others from the Dilaram community and we headed off to church. After a short drive we pulled up outside Kabul Christian Community Church. The large triangular-fronted building with its tall, green pointed roof stood in a large compound, and we walked through the main gates. People were greeting each other as they made their way into the main sanctuary before the service began. Gathering inside the building, we took our seats among diplomats, aid workers and missionaries from Western nations.

Although they were culturally different from our group of rag-tag travellers, they welcomed us warmly and made us feel at home. While they were dressed in their conservative Western clothes, we showed up with our long hair and hippy attire. It was a 'come as you are' church where all were welcome. No judgement, no condemnation, just lots of love and acceptance. Many of them had come to serve the people of Afghanistan, a poverty-stricken nation with a desperate need of development. The entire congregation was made up of expats, and there were no Afghans present that I was aware of. In fact, as far as I knew, there were no Afghan Christians in Afghanistan at this time, and any form of proselytising was strictly forbidden.

It was here that I met the church pastor, Christy Wilson, and his wife, Betty, who had lived in Afghanistan for almost twenty-two years at the time I was there. They were a wonderful, loving, caring couple who exuded God's love for people. I learned that Christy had grown up in Iran, where his parents were missionaries for two decades. In 1951 he arrived on Afghan soil with Betty where they eventually founded Kabul Christian Community Church in their home. This continued until 1970 until they built the church building which I was visiting that day. Permission was given for the construction by the Afghan government under strict conditions that no Afghan would be allowed to attend. This was the only church building that was allowed to exist on Afghan soil.

Afghanistan had not always been hostile to Christianity, however. As far back as the fifth century, Nestorian missionaries travelled through Afghanistan preaching the gospel and establishing churches. Still today, in some patterns on Afghan carpets, one can find small crosses woven into the design dating back to that period. In the 1830s Joseph Wolff, an Anglican clergyman, either rode on horseback or walked through the land preaching the gospel and was able to share his faith with the king and leading Muslim theologians. In the 1850s missionaries began to settle along India's North-West Frontier border with Afghanistan to the east, which is now Pakistan's, as well as Iran's border with Afghanistan to the west where they ministered to Afghans who crossed the borders for medical treatment. In 1951, the country opened its doors to outsiders, and this is when Christy and Betty arrived. They were among the very first foreigners who came into the country.

The church service now began. After only occasionally experiencing a more formal and traditional church service style as a child, to me, this was refreshing. Some hymns were sung and the pastor spoke an encouraging message from the Bible. The whole atmosphere was informal and relaxed. At one point in the service, it was time for communion. I had only seen communion in the more traditional UK churches where people would go to the altar at the front of the church and receive the wafer and wine. Here, small pieces of bread and juice in small cups were passed out to all who were gathered. Pastor Wilson went on to share the meaning of what we were about to do.

I still remember his words as he went on to say that communion was for those who believe in Jesus and had committed their lives to him, as it was an expression of belief in what Jesus had done for us. This didn't come across in an excluding way, but in a way which drew people into an open and welcoming relationship with Jesus. It was an invitation to receive. These words challenged me further to search my own heart to discover where I was at with what I believed at this point in my spiritual journey. I decided that I did believe in Jesus and wanted to follow him. I took communion and felt that this was another step forward on my spiritual journey and a confirmation of my new, emerging belief.

The service ended, and we all went out into the church compound where coffee was being served on a spacious lawn. It was a beautiful, sunny day and the sky was a clear blue. It was now the beginning of November and there was a light coolness in the gentle breeze. I chatted with a few people until it was time to leave. We headed for a waiting taxi, and I climbed into the back seat with two others.

We were just about to drive off when Betty Wilson came running toward us. 'We had a couple of people who would have been joining us for lunch today, but they are unable to make it. Would two of you like to have lunch with us?' I found out that church members regularly invited people from the Dilaram community for lunch after church as a way to give them a sense of home and family. One of the guys from

Dilaram who was sitting in the front seat turned and, pointing to myself and a girl from Finland who was travelling through Kabul and visiting church that morning, said, 'I'm sure these two would love to join you.' We got out of the taxi and joined the Wilsons for lunch.

The Wilsons had a simple but beautiful home, which was set in the church compound and decorated with things they had collected while in Afghanistan. After spending so much time travelling along Eastern roads, and staying in cheap hotels, it felt good to be in a house which, to me, looked and felt very normal. It was a real home. We joined the Wilsons and two other people around the table. It was so interesting to talk over lunch and find out about their unusual, exciting lives as each one shared what had brought them to this unique land.

After lunch, Betty invited the Finnish girl and me into the living room for coffee. We were seated in comfortable chairs. She casually talked with us and showed a genuine interest in our lives. As we continued our conversation, we moved onto things of a more spiritual nature. I began to share where I was at on my own spiritual journey, saying that I believed in God and was open to learn more about him. I basically said I was still searching for the way forward.

At that point, Betty produced a small booklet and asked if I had seen it before. I said that I hadn't. She then asked if she could share some things from it about Jesus. There was definitely no objection from me. In my recent experience in the hotel room, I had prayed that Jesus would somehow reveal himself to me more fully. Then the three German guys, whom I was sharing a room with, were invited to visit a community of Christians. Now I ended up in the home of a pastor and his wife who wanted to talk to me about the reality of Jesus and how I could know him. It was easy to see that all of this was more than a natural coincidence and that God was at work in the details.

Using the small booklet with its simple diagrams, Betty went on to share with us a very simple message of Jesus. She talked about who he was and why he came to this broken world. She talked about the love God has for us and explained how humanity became separated from God, but Jesus came to bridge the gap between God and humankind to restore our relationship with him. All I had to do was receive Jesus into my life and make a commitment to follow him. It was not something I could work for but a gift I could receive.

These words fell into my heart like cool, refreshing water to a man dying of thirst in a hot, dry desert. Everything within me responded with a loud 'yes' to all that she was saying. I had the feeling that I had been lost for so long but had now found my way home. It was like a million voices of heavenly angels were crying out, 'This is the way, this is the truth, this is the end of your search.' Betty paused for a few moments letting the words she had shared sink deep into our hearts and minds. Then, in the silence of the room, she spoke in a soft voice.

'Would you like to receive Jesus and commit your life to him?'

Now another voice broke the silence. It was my own.

'Yes! More than anything else that I could ever desire in this world I want to give my life to Jesus and follow him.'

We bowed our heads and prayed together. The Wilsons' home became sacred ground for me that day where I encountered the eternal God. I felt the darkness over my life was broken and divine light flooded my whole being. A peace I'd never experienced before engulfed my heart. My search ended and I fell into the arms of Jesus.

Before I left the house, Betty gave me a New Testament. It's a little worn now but I still have it with me today and inscribed in the cover are these words:

Presented to Geoff on the day November 5th 1972 that in faith asked Christ into his life. From your brother and sister in Christ.
Christy and Betty Wilson

I left that day with a heart filled with joy. For me, that day was not only the end of a search but a new beginning. I was about to discover that it was the start of an incredible life journey where, as I followed the radical leading of God in my life, I would take some daring steps of faith into unchartered waters and unexpected places where I would see the miraculous hand of God at work in incredible ways. But first, I needed to powerfully encounter the Holy Spirit.

6

Power in High Places

Following my commitment to Christ, I was invited to move into Dilaram House where I could learn more about Jesus and discover the kind of life he now wanted me to live as his disciple. In Matthew 28:18–20 Jesus gave a command to his followers to go into the whole world and make disciples of 'all nations'. A disciple is someone who follows the life and teaching of someone else. In the time of Christ, people were taught by rabbis, some of whom differed in what they taught. It all depended on how they perceived the Jewish law as it was written in the Torah. Jesus came on the scene and was considered to be a rabbi, but with a whole new teaching. In fact, the teaching he brought was so radical that the religious leaders were threatened and enraged by much of what he taught.

His was a message of love and freedom. While the widespread religious teaching of the day was based on law, works and judgement, Jesus appeared on the scene with a message of a God who was reaching out to humanity with passionate love and outrageous grace. He offered new, eternal life to all who would receive it. Where people were oppressed by religion, he came to lift every burden and release humanity from the yoke of oppression. He offered something radically different from anything people had heard before, and as a result, many followed him and listened to what he said. This was not just dogma, or doctrine, but a way of life which, if followed, could radically change the world. And that was his plan, to save the world. His new message was powerful and life-changing. As he gathered a group of followers, he told them to take his message to the nations and make disciples of this way of believing and living.

I moved into Dilaram House and immediately entered into the life of the community where we sought to live out what Jesus taught on a daily basis. Dilaram was very influenced by the Jesus movement of that time, which placed a great emphasis on community living, solid relationships with God and one another, and walking in love towards others. We shared what we had with one another and reached out to those in need. I, like others in the Dilaram community – and like many thousands of others who had come to faith through the Jesus movement – had no church background. I had no concept whatsoever of what it meant to be a Christian. I actually had no idea of what a Christian looked like.

I thank God for those early days when I was mentored in a way that gave me a solid foundation in living out the life and teaching of Jesus. By now, my money that had been stolen had been refunded, and I could have easily moved on to India, which had been my original goal. However, I knew that God wanted me to stay in Kabul so that I could learn more and grow in my relationship with him. I felt that, through Jesus, my search had ended, and I had such a deep peace and contentment in my heart. In my new relationship with God, I knew that he was telling me to stay on and use this time to learn more and grow closer to him.

Life continued, with its daily routines. In some ways, it was like living in a mini Bible school. After breakfast, we would gather for prayer and listen to teaching from the Bible, which was usually taught by Floyd, or one of the other leaders, but occasionally we would listen to teaching on cassette tapes by various speakers. We would also have work that needed to be done around the house, which each of us were assigned to. The cold winter was beginning to set in, and the first snow would soon arrive, so we needed wood for the stoves. I remember chopping wood in the garden as part of my assignment. Some afternoons we would head into the Chicken Street area where we would reach out to those we found in need. For me, it was an enriching, powerful season of change and growth, and some of the lessons I learned still guide my life today. They have certainly guided my ministry over the years.

I longed for more of God in my life. I was like someone who had been starved of food for a long period and had been invited to a banquet. I wanted to eat and eat and eat from the table that God had set out before me. I just couldn't get enough of God and the Bible. I would spend a lot of my free time reading the Bible and praying. I began to underline verses where I felt God was speaking into my life. I found promises I could believe God for, and commands to follow. Not commands which would take away from my life but commands which, when followed, would enrich my life for the better. For instance, Jesus said people would know we were his disciples if we loved one another (John 13:34–35). He said that everything came down to loving God and loving our neighbour (Matt. 22:37–40). Imagine how the world would be a much better place if people followed those commands. I found the Bible to be a book of wisdom which, although written in ancient times, still relates to life today. All this was new to me and I loved every moment of my new life.

In my fresh hunger for God, I read in the New Testament where people were filled with the power of God's Spirit. I especially saw this throughout the book of Acts. I saw that the power of God in the lives of those in the early Church was something which was experiential and brought them into a fresh, powerful walk with God. I also read where Jesus said if anyone was thirsty, they could come to him and drink, and that 'rivers of living water' would flow from their very being (John 7:37–39). He was speaking of the Holy Spirit and I was longing for more of his power in my life. I would pray for long periods, seeking God for more of him.

At that time, my tourist visa for Afghanistan was coming to an end and needed to be renewed. This meant travelling into Pakistan and re-entering Afghanistan on a new tourist visa, which was easy to obtain from Peshawar, the first city in Pakistan when entering from Afghanistan. I planned to leave on a Tuesday, as that was the day my visa expired. The trip involved taking an early morning bus, which would take me through the Kabul Gorge, the mountain range one goes through on leaving the city heading towards the Pakistan border.

During that time, I had become friends with an American missionary family who were based in Kabul and made regular ministry trips into India. Ray and Dorothy had previously lived in India where they travelled with their five children, preaching the gospel to all who would listen to their message. They had moved to Kabul where they settled as a family, and Ray would travel in his vehicle to India where he would conduct evangelistic events, which would attract huge numbers of people.

I knew that Ray and his assistant would be shortly leaving for India via Pakistan. Normally I would have loved to have travelled with them, but in talking to them after church, they said that, due to some problems they were having with the vehicle, they couldn't say when they would be able to leave. They needed some car parts, and special papers that would allow them to travel through Pakistan and into India, but the authorities refused to release them. They were praying that things would work out for them because, like me, they needed to leave soon. I didn't want to take the risk of waiting, as I would be in serious trouble with the authorities if I did not leave the country on the day my visa expired. As I was about to go and purchase my bus ticket, I felt God speak to me. 'Don't purchase a bus ticket, you will be going with Ray.'

This was a bit scary for me. I knew the Bible talked about God speaking to people but all of this was still new to me, and I wondered if this really was God speaking. I knew that if I went over my visa expiration date, there would be serious consequences with the Afghan authorities. I didn't want to take that chance. However, in the end, I decided to follow what I felt God had put in my heart. Learning to hear and follow that voice would take me into some situations in the future where I would only have God's word to stand on and for now, against the odds, I decided to go with what God said.

On Sunday afternoon, following the church service, I was in downtown Kabul in the Chicken Street area. As I was walking down the street I saw Ray's assistant walking towards me. I asked him how things were going with getting everything released for their vehicle. He replied that everything had just been cleared and they would be leaving for India. That was great news but still didn't guarantee that it would get me out of the country on the day I needed to leave, which was in two days' time. I asked him when they were leaving and his reply was Tuesday, the day I had to be out of the country. Wow! I learned again that day that when we know God has said something to us personally, we really can trust his word. Tuesday morning came, they picked me up and we headed out of the city.

It was now January, and winter had set in across Kabul. Snow had fallen on the mountains and over parts of the city.

We headed out along the road that would take us to the city of
Jalalabad from where we would cross the border and travel on
to Peshawar, Pakistan's sixth largest city. While in Peshawar, I
would renew my visa for Afghanistan and head back to Kabul.
I was about to discover why the road from Kabul to Jalalabad
is one of the world's most dangerous roads.

The road we travelled on was classed as a national highway,
but don't think of a modern, wide road. Think more of a winding, twisting mountain road with sections where two cars could
barely pass. We were fortunate to have mild weather, as sometimes the road would get blocked by heavy snowfall. We drove
through great chasms of bare, rugged mountains and cliffs that
were literally breathtaking in their awesome majesty.

However, I was about to discover that some parts of the journey would take my breath away for a different reason. Sections
of the road were incredibly narrow and some of the bends were
impossibly sharp. Then, in some places, there was a possible
fall from the edge of the road of several hundred feet down
a vertical, sheer drop into the fast-flowing river below, which
caused me to literally hold my breath. Vehicles with bald tyres
and screeching brakes would try to overtake us, oblivious to oncoming traffic. In various places I would see a crushed car, bus
or truck lying like a mutilated corpse in the valley below. Large,
colourfully decorated trucks piled high with heavy goods, their
overburdened loads swaying from side to side, would inch their
way around sharp bends.

The only signs of humanity we saw alongside the road were
people living in the impoverished, lonely villages. Looking
at the inhospitable mountains, with their deep, treacherous
passes, I could understand why Afghanistan had always been
so hard to conquer by outsiders. The Afghans, who knew every
crevice and hideaway among these barren, rugged hills, were

no match for those who tried to invade their land. In 1842, the British were defeated and made their retreat from Kabul on this very same road where 17,000 troops and civilians were brutally massacred, their blood spilled across the resilient mountains. Only one lonely British survivor made his way into the city of Jalalabad on horseback.

In the not so scary sections of the journey, I was able to talk to Ray and his assistant and find out more about them and the ministry they were involved with in India. I discovered an area of Christianity I'd never encountered or heard about before. They spoke of healings and miracles and tens of thousands of people coming to hear the good news of the gospel. They spoke of the power of God being manifest through their ministry in the most incredible way, which resulted in many people committing their lives to Christ. When I asked them what brought these dynamics into their ministry, they talked about the power of the Holy Spirit, which was given to fill us, and empower us, so that we could be more effective witnesses for Christ. They went on to say that the Holy Spirit wanted to partner with us in reaching people with the good news that Jesus came to bring.

I discovered that day that the Holy Spirit wanted to fill me and saturate every area of my being. I told them I had been reading in Acts 2 where the first believers were filled, and empowered, with the Holy Spirit and I had been crying out for more of him in my life. I asked these guys what I needed to do to be filled with more of God's Spirit, and their answer was simple. Receive by faith. I asked them if they would pray with me right then and there, and they replied with a positive 'yes'. So, sitting in the back seat of a vehicle, while travelling on one of the world's most ancient and dangerous roads, they prayed for me to be filled with the Spirit of God.

Suddenly it seemed like all of heaven filled the vehicle and then filled me. I felt as though I had been submerged in an ocean of God's presence, power and love, and from deep down inside of me there was an upsurge of ecstatic worship, which overflowed in a beautiful language of praise and adoration to God. Like Moses who had encountered the burning bush (Exod. 3:1–6), I too felt the ground beneath was holy and inhabited by God.

Again, I realised that God didn't need a lofty cathedral or some other designated place of worship, but he can meet us anywhere because he is everywhere present. In Jeremiah 23:24 we read, '"Who can hide in secret places so that I cannot see them?" declares the LORD. "Do not I fill heaven and earth?"' God is everywhere. In Acts 17:28 the apostle Paul said, 'For in him we live and move and have our being.' From that day on, I have always relied on the power, presence and partnership of the Holy Spirit to help me with whatever I've had to face in life, and I have always found him to be a constant friend, helper and guide.

Travelling on, the mountains reduced in size until we approached a dusty plain stretching out before us. This brought us to the city of Jalalabad where we stopped for something to eat before we moved on to the border. We cleared our passports on the Afghan side and, crossing a bleak stretch of land, entered Pakistan. With the checkpoint behind us, we continued our journey which, after a few miles, took us into another mountain range, the famous Khyber Pass, so rich in history. Like other places in the region, this was once an integral part of the Silk Road extending from Shanghai, China to distant Spain. It was also an important trade route between the Indian subcontinent and Central Asia. Camel caravans carrying precious goods would plod their way along this ancient road, and the armies of Cyrus, Darius I, Alexander the Great and Genghis Khan marched along its dusty roads.

This is the land of the fiercely proud and independent Pathan tribes who live across the hills and mountains. Known for its guns, violence and banditry, it has always been recognised as an unsafe place, and along the road we would see signs asking tourists not to wander from the road. As we travelled, it was common to see men carrying rifles, some walking, some on horseback. Hill forts and houses surrounded by high, earth-coloured walls could be seen on the distant hilltops. Journeying on, we passed through the great arch of the Bab-e-Khyber, the great gate and entrance to the Khyber Pass, which covered the road from one side to the other, and we eventually came to Peshawar, one of the world's oldest cities.

It was so refreshing to be in a city that seemed, from all appearances, to be more developed than Kabul. Wide tree-lined streets and boulevards ran in various directions. Being at a lower altitude, the warmth of the winter sun was welcomed after the cold and snow I had just left behind. I said goodbye to the others, who would journey on to India. Calling an auto rickshaw, a three-wheeled vehicle used widely in that part of the world, I climbed inside and headed to the address I'd been given of an English missionary family who accommodated people from Dilaram who came to Peshawar to renew their Afghan visas. After a few days staying with the family and listening to incredible stories of their adventures in this part of the world, I obtained a new visa and headed back to Afghanistan.

I travelled the same route back to Kabul, except this time it was by bus. Arriving at the bus station, I boarded the vehicle and took my place on the back seat. The bus was crowded to full capacity, and its roof was loaded with goods people were carrying home. With the sound of shouts and the roar of the

engine, the old bus pulled out of the station and began its journey into the mountains. If I thought that my journey coming to Peshawar was scary, I was now about to have scariness
multiplied on many levels on my return to Kabul. To begin
with, there had been heavy snowfall in the mountains and the
snow continued to fall as we reached the mountain range of the
Kabul Gorge. In preparation for this, the bus halted and chains
were placed around the tyres.

In any Western nations, I'm pretty sure the road would have
been closed because of the danger of travel. Here it was filled
with traffic moving in both directions in heavy, falling snow
along narrow roads and bends with a drop of hundreds of feet
over the edge. I was seated in the corner of the bus on the back
row behind one of the back wheels. I talked myself into a place
of calm, believing that the driver was experienced with these
conditions so we would be OK. Having said that, the thoughts
of overturned vehicles I'd seen in the valleys below on my previous journey were still fresh in my mind. Because I was sitting
in a rear corner, every time the bus pulled out to the edge of the
road to give access to an oncoming vehicle all I could see, looking down from my window, was a sheer drop below, especially
when we went around a bend.

The bus pulled, chugged and heaved its way up the mountain passes. At one point, as the bus turned a sharp bend, I
looked out of the window viewing the great drop way down to
the valley below. The bus slowly edged around a bend moving
in an upward ascent. Then, with a drop of hundreds of feet, as it
turned there was a sudden jolt as the wheel beneath me slipped
off the edge of the road. Some people gasped, others screamed;
my heart went into overdrive and I thought that this could be a
good time to pray.

Fortunately, the wheel of the bus had positioned itself on a wide ledge of rock that jutted out just inches below the side of the road. Thankfully, because of this, it had only been a slight drop and the driver was able to pull the wheel of the bus back onto the road. Then, as if nothing had happened, everything resumed to the normal chatter and laughter and we went on our way as everyone just took it all in their stride. I thanked God for his protection that day.

7

Persecution and Provision

Returning to the Dilaram community, I discovered a baptismal service was being planned for those who were new Christians. I had only ever understood baptism as something that was for newborn children who were baptised into the Christian faith. I had already been baptised, or christened, as a baby in our local Anglican church. It was explained to me that in the early Church people were baptised after they became Christians, and that this was a symbolic act and witness to others, showing that they had died to their old life and had risen to a new one in Christ. The more I studied verses in the New Testament on baptism, the more I wanted to take this next step on my spiritual journey.

I was ready to do anything I thought would please God and saw this as a step of obedience towards what he was asking me to do. One day I mentioned to one of the guys in the house, who had recently become a Christian, that I had made the decision to be baptised. I think he didn't feel that he was ready to take this step and he challenged me on my decision. He said he thought that maybe I should take more time to think through the commitment involved instead of making what he thought was an emotional, impulsive decision. I actually felt that I had solidly thought this through, had prayed about my decision and believed that this was what God wanted me to do. However, what he said put me in a place of doubt. Maybe I was being impulsive and needed to prove myself more to God and make myself more worthy of baptism.

By now I had been taught to pray about every decision I needed to make. I also knew that I could pray and God would reveal his will, which I believed was important for me to follow. I decided that if God wanted me to be baptised, he could reveal his will, and if he thought I wasn't ready, then I was happy to wait. With my Bible in my hand, I found a quiet place in the house where I could be alone, and while there, I began to pray, asking God to show me his will. I said that I wanted to be baptised but that if he felt I wasn't ready, or was still unworthy, then I needed to know. I was still totally new to seeking God's will, and in a very innocent way, I told God that I would pray over my Bible, open it, and wherever my finger fell that would be his word to me.

In a simple, childlike way I had no doubt about God's ability to speak to me that day. I prayed and randomly opened my Bible and placed my finger on the opened page. The Bible opened at the book of Acts and my finger was on a section in chapter 22, verses 14–16. I began to read, 'The God of our ancestors has chosen you to know his will and to see the Righteous One and to hear words from his mouth. You will be his witness to all people of what you have seen and heard. And now what are you waiting for? Get up, be baptised and wash your sins away, calling on his name.'

This totally blew me away. I could hardly believe how direct this was. Three things stood out to me and seemed to leap from the page like fire and burn into my heart. God has 'chosen' *me*, *I* will be 'his witness to all people' and 'be baptised'. In the silent sacredness of that moment, I felt the call and destiny of God descend upon my life. I knew that, when these verses said 'all people', it meant nations. I knew at that moment that God had called me to preach the gospel to nations and that my life would be lived serving him and following that call. I also sensed that Asia and the Muslim world would be a part of his will for my life. And that settled it. With an open, joyful heart, the decision was sealed and I was ready for this important step of baptism.

It was a crisp, cool day as we headed to church that Sunday morning. The clear blue sky stretching across the heavens above us seemed to radiate the purity and the glory of God. After some hymns and an encouraging word from Pastor Christy, one by one, we shared from our hearts about our journey to Christ. Every story was different but each one emotionally moving. Then, following others, I stepped into the water and, after being placed into its depths, I rose to a new life in Christ. As I came up from the water, the first faces I saw were Christy and Floyd who had baptised me, two men who had put so much into my life, and as I looked across the congregation, I noticed every other face was beaming with so much joy and love.

The memory of Kabul Christian Community Church will always hold a special place in my heart, and I will always re-member the rich times of worship, teaching and fellowship that took place within its walls. Yet, as precious as the building was to us and to God, and as it stood as a great witness to Christ and his cause, none of us could ever have imagined what was about to happen next.

I was visiting the home of some American friends after church one day when the phone rang. This was several weeks after the baptism service. On the other end of the phone, an urgent voice asked us if we could get to the church building as soon as possible. A group of soldiers, led by a few hard-line

Muslim priests (known as 'mullahs' in Afghanistan), were attacking the outside of the compound and breaking down the walls. Their goal was to destroy the church building. Church members were contacting others across the Christian community and asking them to get to the building and pray.

We immediately got into the vehicle and headed for the church. When we arrived, we found soldiers breaking down the outer walls of the compound spurred on by a group of fanatical mullahs. As we headed for the church, I saw several others from Dilaram who had arrived before us. Entering the main sanctuary, there were people across the seated area either sitting or kneeling as they cried out to God in prayer.

As I joined them, I didn't really think of our personal safety. I guess I just believed that God would protect us. One by one we offered up prayer to God. I never heard anyone pray in a negative way towards those outside who were attacking the building. There were no calls for judgement and no bitterness or hatred expressed, but only prayers for forgiveness and for their eyes to be opened to how much God loved them. I thought of the words of Jesus where he said we should bless those who curse us and pray for those who ill-treat us (Luke 6:27–28). He said we should love our enemies, following his example of extending forgiveness to the very people who nailed him to the cross (Matt. 5:44; Luke 23:34).

While we prayed inside, some of the male church members who had served in Afghanistan for a long period of time and spoke the language well tried to talk with those who were attacking the building. Eventually, realising that we would not move from the interior of the church building, they left us, leaving part of the wall damaged. This event brought a dark shadow over the small group of believers who had come to serve the precious people of Afghanistan. As attitudes at high levels of authority changed towards the Christian community, we all wondered what would happen next. A few months later, the Wilsons were given orders to leave the country, and the destruction of the church building was completed. On the day the building was destroyed, a military coup took place that deposed King Mohammed Zahir Shah, ending his forty years' reign.

After spending almost five months in Afghanistan, I began to sense my time there was coming to an end. This whole period had been rich and life-changing, but I knew I could not stay there forever. The Bible says life happens in seasons – Ecclesiastes 3:1 says, 'There is a time for everything, and a season for every activity under the heavens'.

As the seasons change in nature, so we also must move on through the various seasons of our lives. Nothing stays the same. God has seasons for each one of us and, as we walk with him, we can learn to discern each new season that he brings us into. This does not happen suddenly, but as in nature, each season evolves through transition, beginning with a stirring in the heart for new direction and allowing a time of preparation for what is to happen next. I was beginning to discern that this season of my life journey was ending and it was time for me to move on.

Now my life had radically changed and I needed to figure out the way forward. I prayed and asked God what he wanted for my future. I knew I needed God to give me a vision for my life's call. I needed to know what his plan was for me so that I could prepare for the next step and for my future. My life was now his, and I felt that I wanted to return to England and spend time waiting on God in anticipation for whatever he had planned for the next part of my life's journey.

Being in Afghanistan had placed a great desire in my heart to reach unreached nations with the good news of Jesus. I became a Christian in a strongly Islamic, unreached nation where very few had heard the gospel, and I had enjoyed rich fellowship among a people whose commitment to Christ had brought them from their birth countries to serve Jesus in a distant land. Apart from the guy I had met on Oxford Street, London, I had never had a strong connection with any other Christians, and even he was an American missionary to the UK.

My whole basis in becoming a Christian was to say 'yes' to the call of God to follow Jesus and commit to going in obedience to wherever he would lead. Jesus drew me to himself and asked me to follow him, and missions was burned into my heart right at the very start. I prayed and dedicated my whole self to God, telling him that I didn't feel that I had a lot of ability but I offered him my availability. I went on to let God know my heart, that I would go anywhere he wanted me to go, would say anything he wanted me to say, and would do whatever he wanted me to do. And although I felt some sadness at leaving this beautiful land, I knew in my heart, without any shadow of doubt, that I would return to Asia to bring good news to those who have never heard.

The day neared when several of us were leaving and heading West. Some would be joining a YWAM school in Lausanne, Switzerland, but I would travel on to the UK. We booked our bus tickets from Kabul to Herat from where we would cross the border into Iran and journey on to Europe. This would take us back on the same route we had all travelled and which had brought us to Kabul, where each of us had found new life in Christ. For me there was just one problem. The money I had refunded from my stolen traveller's cheques had run out, and I didn't have the money I needed to get from Herat to England. This was a time to trust God. Right up until the day we were due to leave, I didn't have the money to make the trip.

On the morning of departure, Floyd approached me with some news. Early on that very morning, someone had come to the house and said God had spoken to him and his wife in the night. He said God had told them to take some money to Dilaram House which would be enough for one person on the team who needed it to travel to Europe. Floyd handed me all the cash I needed to get back to England. I was amazed.

We said our goodbyes to the others and boarded the bus. As the bus pulled out of the station, I said goodbye to Kabul, the city that had become so dear to my heart and where so much had taken place in my life. With the mountains and deserts behind us, we travelled west. I was returning to the UK a changed person. I didn't know it at the time, but my stay in England would be much shorter than expected.

8

Learning to Hear God's Voice

The cold spray from the sea blew against my face as the ferry ploughed its way through the turbulent waters below. I had just left Calais, France and was now heading home. I strained my eyes to gaze through the mist that had settled over the waters. In the far distance I saw a shape begin to form and, as things became clearer, I saw what I was looking for.

The great white cliffs of Dover, England, rising 350 feet above the sea, were in my sight. I thought of what these cliffs had meant to people over the years. To invaders like the Romans, and others, they would be the completion of a journey to a land that they would pillage and conquer. To others who had fought in, and survived, some of the most horrific wars known to humankind, they would be a welcome home. For me, they meant a return to the land of my birth, and a return as a person who was totally changed from the one who had left these shores several months earlier. I wondered what my new life here would be like.

From Dover, I travelled across England to reach my parents' home in the north of England. After spending time in Afghanistan, with its barren deserts and mountains, England was a feast of rich colour and changing scenery. I journeyed north past green, rolling hills with fields spreading out in every direction. Here and there towns would appear and small, picturesque country villages nestled in ageless vales with ancient church steeples rising heavenwards could be seen in the distance.

My parents were so pleased to see me after such a long time and, after I had sent them letters in which I shared with them about the new direction my life had taken, they were eager to discover more about my new-found faith and the changes which had come into my life as a result. I settled into my parents' home and began my search for a church which I could attend. This was a totally new experience for me, and I asked God to lead me to the right place. I had heard of a small evangelical church near my parents' home and walked there one Sunday morning. I knew the service would already be underway but wanted to check the outside of the building to see if there was a noticeboard giving more information on the church. I also wanted to try to get a feel about the place and ask God if this was where I should be.

As I had previously thought, the service inside was already underway when I arrived. As I looked at the noticeboard outside the church, the door to the building opened and an older lady came out. On seeing me, she asked if she could be of help. I told her a little about myself and how I had recently become a Christian. She went on to explain that while in the church service she felt the Holy Spirit asked her to go outside, something she would never usually do. At the exact moment I was outside she came out of the building. She introduced herself and invited me into the building where, at the end of the service, I met other members of the church.

I eventually settled into church life but was so restless. I think some of it was a natural reaction to where I had found myself. After living life on the edge for the past few years in

London and then Afghanistan, I found it difficult to settle into a semi-rural, small community steeped in conservative English life. While that was a natural reaction, my spiritual reaction was that I had a burning desire in my heart to reach people with the good news of Jesus. I must admit that coming from a totally different background, I struggled to fit into UK church life. My whole Christian experience was living with a very close-knit community of people where we shared life together on a daily basis. Because I was used to that, it took me some time to adjust to a new way of living.

Added to that was the fact that I had become a Christian in one of the world's most unreached areas. No one had heard the gospel in Afghanistan – except, perhaps, a small handful of people. I had lived among Muslims and missionaries. I had seen first-hand the unreached masses spread out before me. A burden for missions was birthed in my heart and travelling across Afghanistan, when passing by villages along the road, I would drop gospel tracts from the bus window, hoping people would read them and discover Jesus.

I had also been immersed in a Christianity where world-reaching missions was the normal way of life and service. I had seen the needs of nations like Turkey, Iran, Afghanistan and Pakistan and knew that many other lands beyond their borders were waiting to hear of the amazing Jesus I had come to know. My desire to reach unreached people with the good news, and be involved in full-time missions, continued to grow.

In the meantime I did what I could where I was. I met some other young people and we gathered together to pray and reach out to others wherever we could. The result was that we saw more young people give their lives to Jesus. I knew, though, that God had called me to missions, and Bible verses that spoke of God's heart for the nations continually spoke to my heart. I knew that in his final words, Jesus commissioned his disciples to 'go and make disciples of all nations' (Matt. 28:18–20). These were his final words to his disciples in which he expressed his heart, vision and desire for the lost humanity of this world. I felt his heart for the nations of the earth and longed to do more.

The months passed and I continued to pray and seek God. I was like a wild horse chomping at the bit and ready to go. Every time I heard a sermon, or read a book or magazine on missions, my heart would cry out to God, asking him to make a way for me to go. As I was praying one day, I heard the 'gentle whisper' of God (1 Kgs 19:12) speak to my heart asking me to prepare to return to Asia. As wonderful as this was, I felt both excited and nervous at the same time.

First of all, I wondered if this really was God's word to me or just my imagination. Then, the realisation of how major a decision this would be was pretty scary, and added to that was that I just didn't know what I should do next. I decided to wait on this, give it more time and continue to seek God concerning the next step. Proverbs 3:5–6 says, 'Trust in the LORD with all your heart and lean not on your own understanding; in all your ways submit to him, and he will make your paths straight.' I decided to commit my way to God and trust him to work it all out.

I had learned by now that we are not left to figure out life's direction by ourselves, but we have a relationship with God who has promised to lead us and guide us throughout life's journey. I knew there were many verses in the Bible that spoke of God's promise to guide us into his will.

Ephesians 5:17 encourages us to 'not be foolish, but understand what the Lord's will is.' I leaned on verses like Psalm 32:8 which says, 'I will instruct you and teach you in the way you should go; I will counsel you with my loving eye on you.' I knew from this verse that God loved me and would direct me. Then in the tenth chapter of John's gospel, Jesus speaks of his sheep hearing his voice (v. 27). Reading these and other verses gave me the encouragement I needed to know that God would guide me and show me the way forward.

However, trying to discern God's will was not easy. I knew that God had called me to missions and that the area he had called me to was Asia, but I was unsure what steps I should take next to respond to that call. I needed more specific guidance as to where exactly God was calling me, so I began to pray for more confirmation and clearer direction.

I talked to my pastor at that time but, I think, he didn't know what to do with me or how to advise me. I hadn't been a Christian very long, so didn't have a lot of Bible knowledge or experience in any kind of Christian ministry. Added to that, the church I attended didn't really have any kind of interest in overseas missions or a commitment towards that. So, basically, it was me and God. I committed all of this into God's hands and waited on him to show me the way.

I continued to wait on God, and my heart remained fixed on what I believed God had said. The problem was that I didn't receive much encouragement from any other direction so, while my heart said it was God's will, my head was sometimes full of doubt thinking that I'd probably made the whole thing up. I prayed that God would confirm his will through other sources.

I knew that God would always confirm his will through the Bible. Sometimes while reading the Bible, certain verses can just stand out to us. At other times, God can whisper a verse of scripture to us while in prayer. This happened to me one day when I was praying and asking God for a confirmation of what he had put in my heart. While praying, 1 Kings 17:2–4 was impressed on my heart. I wasn't sure what was written there so turned to the verses and read, 'Then the word of the LORD came to Elijah: "Leave here, turn eastward and hide in the Kerith Ravine, east of the Jordan. You will drink from the brook, and I have instructed the ravens to supply you with food there."' The words 'leave here and turn eastward' seemed pretty clear, and as I was wondering how I would be financially supported, the mention of God's supernatural provision encouraged me.

In ways like this, God encouraged me when I prayed and read the Bible. One thing that was becoming clear, though, was that as I prayed for clearer direction, the nation that I kept being drawn to was India. Whenever I prayed over a world map, India seemed to stand out from other nations. I kept all of this in my heart and continued to pray.

During this period, Floyd was in England, speaking in churches and other gatherings. Floyd had now established Dilaram communities in New Delhi, India and Kathmandu, Nepal, and had recently moved to Amsterdam with a vision to pioneer a Dilaram community at what was one of the starting routes of the hippy trail. Amsterdam, in the late sixties and early seventies, was a major gathering place for hippies from all across Europe and America. The city's 'anything goes' attitude and tolerance towards the drug culture attracted many who were looking for greater freedom.

While Floyd and his wife, Sally, were in Holland, they were offered the use of two very large houseboats, which were situated right behind the central train station in the centre of Amsterdam. Able to accommodate around forty people, the boats contained sleeping areas for couples and singles, a kitchen, a dining room and a large room that could be used as a coffee bar and a space for bigger gatherings. It was perfect for their needs, and they moved in with the rest of the team.

While one of the boats was called *Jonah*, the other boat, which was used for a coffee bar and Sunday gatherings, was called *The Ark*. They immediately began outreach into the city.

While Floyd was in England, I was unable to visit him, but I phoned one evening just to catch up. I shared with him about where I was at in this period of my life and told him what I felt God had been saying to me. He immediately became excited about what I was saying. 'Hey,' he said. 'One of the reasons why I'm in England is to recruit new workers to help us. We desperately need people to help with our ministry in New Delhi, India.' He went on to say, 'You were with us in Afghanistan and you understand the hippy culture so why don't you pray about going? We would love to have you join the team there.' Although I told him I would pray about it and get back to him, deep down inside I knew that this was a door God had opened and that I needed to make plans to go through it. This was his direction for the next step in my life.

As I continued to pray about all of this, I remember two other things that took place at that time. After talking with Floyd, I visited some friends in the Birmingham area. While there, I went with them to a house church that they were a part of. I hadn't told any of them about what I felt God was calling me to do. At this time, the main thing I was constantly struggling with was that I felt totally inadequate for what I believed God was calling me to. I'd been a Christian for less than two years when all of this was happening.

A group of people were present in the living room of the leader's home. After spending some time worshipping God, a deep, sacred silence fell upon the small gathering. No one spoke or moved. There was a sense that God was about to speak. I was still wrestling with how I felt when the group leader and one of the other guys came over to me and, placing their hands on my shoulders, uttered these words, 'I have called you and chosen you to work for me. Do not look to your own ability but look to my ability working in you. Have I not chosen the weak things of this world to confound those who are wise? I am sending you to distant lands where I will give you a ministry to both those who know me and those who are lost.'

Following this, I attended a large Christian conference. You would almost think that by now I would have been pretty solid in how I felt about all of this, but as I stood among more than three thousand people worshipping God, I still had doubts. I decided to ask God just one more time for a final confirmation. I said to God that I wanted him to do one more thing.

'OK, God,' I said. 'You know my heart. I have had very little encouragement from others when I have shared with them what I feel you are asking me to do. I have been told I am too young, I'm too inexperienced, I don't have enough Bible knowledge. The list can go on and on. Please let someone here give a prophetic word that speaks directly to my heart and I promise that I will seal the deal. Whatever it takes, I'll go for it.'

Immediately, as I finished my prayer, someone stood before the thousands of worshippers believing that God had given them a word for someone in the congregation. I still remember the words that echoed across the auditorium. The message was clear, short and simple: 'Do not say you are inexperienced. You shall go to whom I send you, and I will enable you to do the work that I have called you to do for me.' And that was it. My decision was made. I was now about to embark on a journey into the unknown with nothing to rely on except God himself, a journey in which my faith would be tested on every level.

9

Red Lights and Crack Houses

The dark skies of autumn cast their shadows across the city as sharp, cold winds blew along the narrow streets and canals dislodging brown, gold and rust-coloured leaves from the trees. It was October 1974, and I was now in Amsterdam, where I'd moved onto *The Ark*. I arrived, with very little luggage, and I remember Floyd greeting me and asking me if I was taking the words of Jesus literally where he said to 'take nothing for the journey' (Luke 9:3)! I would be here for a few months before joining the Dilaram community in New Delhi.

We lived just off the centre of old Amsterdam with its narrow, cobbled streets and quaint Lilliputian houses running along the edges of canals. Miniature bridges curved their way across the waterways and steeples of ancient churches, soaring high above, sent out a melodic symphony as church bells rang out onto the streets below. Many tourists visited Amsterdam to experience its beauty and charm.

However, for some, behind the beauty and charm lay a world of corruption, exploitation and damaged lives, and this was the world we came to know. Because we lived in central Amsterdam, we were just a short walk away from the city's famous red-light district. We would watch this Jekyll and Hyde community transform itself from what looked like a normal,

everyday neighbourhood through the day, into a dark under-
world where drugs and prostitution became the norm at night.
This area became one of our places of outreach. While many
came here to be entertained by what they saw, or to pay for sex,
what they didn't see was the damaged, broken lives of many of
the women who were fighting to survive lives of abuse, control
and drug addiction.

Following the vision of Dilaram, the ministry of *The Ark*
continued to reach out to hippies and other countercultural
people in Amsterdam with the good news of Jesus. The people
we wanted to reach were those who would probably never be
contacted by churches, would probably never darken the doors
of a church building, and sadly, in some cases may not even be
welcome. In order to reach them, we needed to go where they
were. Walking the streets of Amsterdam, our world became
one of touching the lives of hippies, criminals, junkies, drug
dealers, prostitutes, runaways and many others who had made
Amsterdam their home. Like Jesus, who was called a 'friend
of . . . sinners' (Matt. 11:19), we followed his lead. This was
definitely no ordinary church outreach.

The Ark and *Jonah* were two large boats that were connected
together and housed an open community of people where anyone could come and learn more about Jesus. Not so much
an introduction to a religion, but more of an invitation to a
relationship with God through Christ. This would also involve
becoming his follower, building a lifestyle on what he taught
and entering a relationship with him that would bring about
healing, wholeness and transformation. We saw the transforming power of God in so many people as they opened up to him
and let him bring salvation and healing into their lives.

On Sunday evenings, we had an open service where people
gathered to worship and receive teaching from the Bible. These

gatherings were very informal, and were mostly attended by young people. We met in the same room that was used as a coffee bar through the week, and sat on cushions on the floor around low tables. In many ways the service was pretty laid back, with an emphasis on being a community of people who sought to love God and love people. This was a great environment for the people we were seeking to reach; they could come just as they were and find love and acceptance. Knowing what many of the people we were reaching out to had been through, we always gave them time to move at their own pace. Some of them became Christians and went on to live lives dedicated to following Jesus.

Through the week we had various programmes going on at *The Ark* and across the city. Shortly after my arrival I was talking to someone about Jesus, and this person gave their life to Christ. As a result of that, Floyd asked if I would lead an evangelism team. This meant reaching out to people across Amsterdam. Along with other team members, our ventures into the city would take us to all kinds of places, mostly among hippies and other countercultural people, where we would visit coffee shops, crack houses and venues where young people would congregate.

Crack houses were buildings that squatters had taken over. Some of the larger buildings were very well-organised in what they did. In one place we would visit a school building which had been taken over by squatters, and every evening they would sell snack-type food and drinks to music played from a sound system. They had quite a thriving small business, which they used to support themselves.

Other places were not as sophisticated. I remember going to a broken-down building which didn't have electricity or any form of heating. It was winter, and the whole building was cold and damp and had a strong, musty smell. It was dusk and the inside of the building was very dark. In one place, I had to make my way along a narrow corridor and, because there were no windows, the area was in total blackness. Feeling my way along in the dark, I stumbled on what I thought was a pile of rags against the wall. They were damp and gave off a foul smell. When I heard someone groan, I realised that under the rags was a doped-up addict. I couldn't believe the condition some people found themselves in. We continued to reach out to people wherever we could; thank God that some people made it to a new life in Jesus. Drugs were openly used in all of the crack houses we visited.

We also visited other large venues in Amsterdam that attracted hundreds of countercultural people. Although these venues often had live bands or loud music playing in one section of their buildings, there were other areas that were more laid back and quiet where we could meet lots of people. This gave us the opportunity to share our faith and invite people back to *The Ark*.

We would always pray and ask God to lead us to the people he wanted us to reach. I remember seeing a guy in one of the venues we visited and felt led to go and talk with him. Our conversation moved on to talking about spiritual things, and I told him that I was a Christian. He immediately began to tell me about what had happened a few nights previously.

He was living in a small room in one of the crack houses, and had used some drugs. On a coffee table next to his bed was a burning candle, and there were other items scattered across the table. As his eyes became heavy and began to close, he lay down on the bed and drifted into a deep sleep. He lay there for some time until he was awakened by the smell of smoke and the sound of crackling flames. The candle had fallen, and now the whole table top was on fire. He quickly put out the flames and saw that everything on the table was completely destroyed except for one thing which had survived intact: the Bible his grandmother had given him. His heart was so open as I shared with him of how Jesus could change his life. After that, he began to visit *The Ark* on a regular basis.

Another time I was in a coffee shop when I felt the Holy Spirit ask me to go and talk with a guy who was sitting a short distance from me. When he began to speak, I could tell by his accent that he was from the north of England. When I asked him where he was from, it turned out that he had always lived just a few miles from my parents' home in the area where I had grown up. I was astounded that, out of all of the people in the crowded city of Amsterdam, God would guide me to someone who was born, and had lived, just a short distance from where I had grown up. That broke the ice, and I was able to have a meaningful conversation with him. In ways like this, God would lead us to people.

During that time, we would see the hand of God provide for us in ways that you would not think were big on God's agenda. Another area I was involved with on *The Ark* was a crafts ministry. The crafts ministry was situated in the basement of an old terraced house in the city and was set up as a way to help rehabilitate people who had come to live with us from a drug lifestyle. Often those from this lifestyle hadn't held down regular jobs and came from an unstructured background lacking any form of discipline. The crafts ministry gave people the opportunity to get into some form of disciplined routine, which would help them transition into a more structured lifestyle and prepare them for a more normal working life.

Several mornings each week, we would head out to the basement in an old minibus and would spend several hours printing cards and making other gifts which would be sold in the small gift shop on *The Ark*. None of us on the crafts team were well-off financially, so we were very careful with whatever money we had. One cold, damp, winter morning, we piled into the minibus and headed out across the city to the crafts workshop. Holland is famous for its Dutch coffee, and there was one particular luxury brand that was way beyond our price range. We were all coffee drinkers, but at the crafts workshop we used a cheaper brand of tea. On the way there, one of the guys said how wonderful it would be if, for just one day, we could get to drink this particular brand of luxury coffee. We all laughed and thought nothing more about it.

Arriving at our destination, we went down the steps to the basement workshop and to our amazement, sitting on the doorstep outside our front door, was a packet of the very coffee we had just been talking about. We never got to know how it got there, but that day we realised that God is even interested in the small things which relate to our lives.

As much as I enjoyed my time in Amsterdam, I knew that it was now coming to an end. I had known that I would only be there for several months before heading out to New Delhi where I would join the Dilaram team. There were two other guys on *The Ark* who, like me, were there for a short period of time before going to work in the Delhi Dilaram community. We began to meet together to pray and plan for the overland trip we would make to India. As Iran and Afghanistan were still open to travellers at that time, our journey would follow the same overland route I had taken on my previous trip. However, this time I was going as a completely different person. We set a leaving date that gave us a few weeks to prepare for our departure.

Just after we made our decision to go, we were in one of our morning gatherings where we would pray and worship, and

Floyd would brief us on updates or give other important information. Usually this would involve anywhere from around thirty to forty people. On this particular morning, he asked us to pray about a specific amount of money, which *The Ark* needed for its heating system. We actually ended up with no heating on either of the boats, and because it was extremely cold, we needed to see the money come in urgently.

As we prayed, it occurred to me that I had the exact same amount of money in my savings that we were praying for. While I had been in England, I had had a temporary job to earn money and had lived as frugally as possible so that I could save up, knowing that one day God would release me to go to the mission field. I knew that whatever money I could save would help me get there.

Over the next few days, we all prayed and expected the money to come in, but nothing showed up. By now I already knew that I was the one who was supposed to give the money, but I held out. I actually debated the issue with God. 'Look, God,' I said. 'I have no financial support from any source. If I give all of my savings away, I will have nothing left.' It just didn't seem fair that after living so frugally to save it, God would ask me to give it away. After all, it was *my* money.

Following the traditional path of most missionary organisations, Dilaram did not pay a salary, but each person was responsible for raising their own financial support. My problem was that I had come from a small church that had offered no financial support, and I had no other way of raising the money I needed. I knew that my savings would get me to India and cover my time there for at least one year, and I was placing my security in that rather than choosing to trust God. As God dealt with my heart, I began to see that he wanted me to place my total trust in him and make him my security. I yielded to what I felt God was asking me to do and handed the whole amount of my savings over. When I finally made the decision, I was filled with peace and was able to do it joyfully.

At this time, I had been reading many books on the lives of missionaries and others who God had used in his service. I read about people like Hudson Taylor, the great missionary to China and founder of the China Inland Mission, and George Müller, whose orphanages were supplied financially by his faith. One thing that struck me was that both of these men had made a commitment to not make their financial needs known to anyone but God, and they trusted him to provide.

I felt I should follow their example of trusting God and not making my financial needs known. I decided that if God had really called me, then he would provide all that I needed. I was due to leave for India soon, where I would spend the coming months or possibly years, and now there was no way, naturally speaking, that I could cover the cost of my travel or sustain myself while I was there. I didn't even have the money to buy the bus ticket for the first leg of the journey. The guys I was travelling with had no idea about my situation. I was totally penniless and wondered how God would provide what I needed for the journey.

There were several buses travelling out of Amsterdam to various destinations across Europe and a few long-haul buses which made the journey out to India. As we wanted to make our own way overland, we decided on a bus company which would take us to Greece, and from there we would make our way east, through Turkey, on local transport. We went to the small travel shop which was located on a side lane just off Dam Square in central Amsterdam. After making enquiries, we decided we would travel with them and return later to purchase tickets that would take us to the northern Greek city of Thessaloniki. From there we would take a train to Istanbul while the bus continued to its final destination of Athens.

Every day I checked my letter box expecting to find an envelope with the amount of money I needed inside, but day after day nothing arrived. This really was a time to trust God. As the day was growing near for us to purchase our tickets, I still didn't have the money I needed. The guys I was travelling with still did not know that I didn't have it, and as we met to pray, I just acted like everything was OK. Although I knew in my heart that God would provide, I still felt anxious at times, especially as we grew nearer to the day when we would have to purchase our tickets.

Philippians 4:6–7 was a great comfort to me. It says, 'Do not be anxious about anything, but in every situation, by prayer and petition, with thanksgiving, present your requests to God. And the peace of God, which transcends all understanding, will guard your hearts and your minds in Christ Jesus.' Whenever I began to feel anxious, I would bring the situation to God and his peace would return. I knew that if he called me to do something for him, he would provide. After all, a little further in Philippians 4:19 we read, 'And my God will meet all your needs according to the riches of his glory in Christ Jesus.' I placed my total trust in God.

It was Sunday evening and the service on *The Ark* had ended. During the service my thoughts would drift towards my financial need, but I chose to focus on worshipping God. I needed money as the next day we were going to buy our bus tickets. Instead of days we were now down to hours. As people dispersed from *The Ark*, my friend Barry Manson walked over to see me before he left. Barry and his wife, Linda, were living in Haarlem, which was a short distance from Amsterdam. He was from Northern Ireland and Linda from the north of England.

After becoming a Christian, Barry began visiting *The Ark* and we became good friends. He knew that I would shortly be leaving for India but had no idea about my financial situation. He asked me if I was free to come to their home in Haarlem one evening for dinner before I left Amsterdam. I said that I would love to come and spend some time with him and Linda, and we fixed a date.

Before leaving, he handed me a white envelope. I didn't know what was inside but thanked him. Later, I opened the envelope and discovered more than enough money to purchase my bus ticket the next day. It was actually about one-third of the amount I needed for the whole trip to India. With a heart filled with joy, I thanked God for his incredible provision. The next day we headed to the travel shop and purchased our tickets. Seeing God provide like that was exciting, but I still needed the remaining amount to cover the rest of the trip. I decided that, if I needed to, I would just get on the bus and believe God to provide along the way. However, God had a different plan.

A few days later I jumped on a train and headed over to Haarlem, where I spent the evening with Barry and Linda. We had a great time together and continued to forge a friendship that has lasted throughout our lives. Linda was out of the room and had left Barry and me to talk. While we were in the middle of our conversation, Barry got up from his chair and said there was something he needed to do. Walking across the room and opening his writing desk, he began to write on a piece of paper, and turning to me, he handed me a cheque. He said that he had felt God tell him he should give it to me. I was amazed. The amount on the cheque was the same amount he had given me in the previous envelope. I now had two-thirds of the money that I needed to cover my travel expenses.

I thanked him and we continued talking. During the conversation, once again, he got up from his chair, went to the writing desk, and said he needed to do something. This was getting crazy. Again, opening his writing desk he began to write on a piece of paper and, once again, turning to me he handed me another cheque and said that God had told him he should give it to me. I looked at the amount written on the cheque and saw that it was the same as the last one. I now had the exact amount I needed to make the trip to India. I could barely believe what had just happened, and even today I get totally blown away by God's supernatural provision whenever it happens. Once again, I learned that God may show up at the last minute, but he is never late.

So that was it. We were ready to go, and on a cold, crisp spring morning in Amsterdam, we all gathered outside *The Ark*, and following prayers and hugs, we said goodbye. Then, walking a short distance along a city street, we climbed inside the bus and headed out of the city. We didn't know it at the time, but the bus we were travelling on would soon come to a sudden, unexpected halt.

10

In the Land of Gods and Gurus

The minibus we were travelling in looked well-used and would seat around fifteen people. It had made many trips to Greece and back. There was an assortment of people inside. Our little group consisted of three Hare Krishna devotees who were also on their way to India, two American girls who were into New Age thought and were studying dreams at a university in Switzerland, a Scottish guy who was on his way to live in a cave in Crete, and a wiry, edgy, jumpy driver who seemed to be living on his nerves. Oh, and we three budding missionary evangelists who were eager to share our faith with those on board and were delighted by the fact that they would not be able to leave the bus for several days. What an opportunity. It did concern me, though, that there was only one driver to cover the whole trip, and there were no plans to stop for any long period anywhere along the way. This was going to be an interesting journey.

As we travelled, we started talking and made an effort to get to know one another better. Obviously, with three Hare Krishna devotees, and the two girls being into New Age thinking, the conversation got round to spiritual topics, which led to talking about belief in God. The three 'spiritual' groups travelling together all had strong, but different, beliefs. As we three guys shared about our faith in Jesus, we experienced some hostility from the group; nothing major, but you could feel the tension, which arose from their negative feelings towards Christianity. I sensed that some of them had not had a positive experience with Christianity or church, so we prayed for an opportunity to share God's love with them.

We crossed the border into Germany and headed towards Switzerland where we would drop the two girls off at their destination and we would continue our journey to Greece. It was now approaching midnight, and as we travelled, the minibus began to make weird noises, and it was clear that there was some kind of problem. As we were skirting the edge of a small town, the driver pulled the vehicle off the side of the road so that he could take a look at the bus. Before he could bring the vehicle to a stop, it decided to come to a halt all by itself and, becoming silent, gave up all signs of life. In searching for the problem, the driver discovered that a major part in the vehicle needed to be replaced. This would mean getting it to a garage where they could replace the part and fix the vehicle, but this was Saturday evening and there would be nowhere open for business on the Sunday. We would just have to sit it out until Monday morning. At this point, everyone started complaining, and the general mood went down. I and the other two Christians decided to pray and trust God to work everything out. By now we were all tired and tried to get some sleep.

The next morning we all woke up from a fitful night's sleep and got out of the vehicle. As it was now light, we could see the area more clearly, and I noticed that we were on the edge of a built-up residential neighbourhood. We had all brought food for the journey, so we settled into different places along an area of grass and had breakfast. I felt that I wanted to be alone and pray so moved away from the others. As I prayed, I sensed that

God wanted to do something special, and I decided to believe that he had a much greater plan in all of this. I had taken my Bible with me and began to read Psalm 23. When I got to verse 5, I read, 'You prepare a table before me in the presence of my enemies.' I thought of the hostility and rejection of our message that we had received from the others on the bus and sensed that God was saying that he would spread a table before us. I took this to have a figurative meaning and felt that God wanted to do something special in answer to our prayers which would be a powerful witness to the others. Throughout the day, I kept thinking of the words 'You prepare a table before me' and wondered what God was going to do.

The morning went on and by now it was lunchtime. Being Sunday I thought of how wonderful it would be to attend a church where we could worship God and have fellowship with other believers. I felt this was something we needed at that time, something we could draw strength and encouragement from. The more I thought about it, the more the desire grew in me to see if there was a church somewhere in the small town.

I asked the other two guys if they would like to join me in looking for a church and said that maybe we could trust the Holy Spirit to lead us to the right place. They agreed and we set off walking. Every time we came to a crossroads, we asked the Holy Spirit if we should go left, right or straight on. Then, we would all agree on which way we should go and took the direction we felt was the correct one. After a number of twists and turns along various streets, we came to what looked like a church building. On the noticeboard outside the building we could see no evidence of an evening service but felt that God must have brought us here for a reason. We noticed an annex at the side of the church building, which looked like it had some-one living in it. We approached the door and rang the bell.

We heard a noise inside, and as the door opened, a woman appeared before us and asked, in German, if she could help. We introduced ourselves and told her that we were Christians from the UK and were on our way to India to do missionary work. Before we could continue with our introduction, she became very excited and began to address us in English with a Scottish accent. She was so overjoyed to meet us and invited us into the home where she lived with her husband. She began to tell us her story of how she had recently married and followed her husband to live here in Germany. That week she had felt extremely homesick and had prayed, asking God to send her some English-speaking Christians with whom she could have fellowship. This was amazing to her and to us. I thought of how God passionately cares for us as individuals and how far he was willing to go to answer the cry of this dear woman's heart.

It doesn't end there. We asked if the church had an evening service. She said that the church only had a Sunday evening service once a year, when they challenged their young people with the needs of overseas missions, and this just happened to be the night. And here we were, three young people, working with a youth organisation, who were heading out to the mission field and had shown up at their young people's missions service. Totally amazing. All I could think of was how incredible God is. We told her all about the breakdown of the bus, of the others we were travelling with, and said that we'd spent the night in the vehicle. She immediately responded by asking us to bring the others to the church that evening and promised to find us all somewhere to sleep.

We went back to the bus, and we told the others what had happened and said that the people in the church would find us somewhere to sleep. That evening we headed back to the church and had the most awesome time, sharing our testimonies with all the young people who had gathered. The people were so warm and welcoming towards the others from the bus and, after the service, we were led into a large room in the basement of the church where places had been set up for us all to sleep. And as I looked across the room, I saw a long table covered with an incredible amount of food that church members had brought for us to eat. With great emotion, and a thankful heart, I thought of what I had read that morning. God had indeed prepared a table for us that evening. I couldn't find enough words to thank God and those precious people.

One of the men in the church asked our bus driver what type of vehicle the bus was and what he thought was causing the problem. He was the manager of a garage in the town that was the main Mercedes-Benz dealership. It just so happened that the bus we were travelling in was a Mercedes-Benz vehicle, and the garage had the part we needed. Even though it was Sunday and the garage was closed, he showed up with a mechanic and completed the work of repairing the bus so we could leave early the next morning. When the driver asked for the invoice, the guy who had organised the repairs said he was happy to do it free of charge. The love that these people showed touched the people on the bus deeply, and they were totally different towards us after that. God touched each of them in a way that opened their eyes and hearts in a greater way to him, and we were able to share with them more openly what we believed.

We travelled into Switzerland where, at one section, the mountain roads were blocked because of heavy snow, and we had to place the vehicle on a train that took us through tunnels cut through the mountains. After dropping the girls off and travelling many more miles, we eventually came to our destination of Thessaloniki, Greece, where we arrived at the train station in the early hours of the morning. From there we caught a train to Istanbul and continued our travels across Turkey and Iran. It felt good to be travelling along the roads I had previously taken, and the whole journey brought back lots of memories. After entering Afghanistan we made our way to Kabul where we stayed for a few days. It was such a blessing to meet up with people I had not seen since I had given my life to Christ in that city. And this time I returned as a missionary myself. After some days, we travelled across Pakistan and eventually reached India.

Crossing the border from Pakistan into India, I was immediately hit with the vibrancy and colour of that nation. We were now in the Indian Punjab, the land of the Sikhs, and in every direction I looked, I was surrounded by an array of multicoloured turbans. The freedom of women on the streets was also noticeable after travelling though Islamic nations. I was so excited to be here, and instantly felt at home in this great land. The first major city we entered in India was Amritsar, the home of the gold-covered Golden Temple, which is sacred to Sikhs and a major place of pilgrimage for people of that religion.

While I was in Afghanistan, I had met with Ray's family, and they told me that he was holding an evangelistic event in Jalandhar, which is the next major city after Amritsar. I went to spend a few days with Ray and his team while the other two guys went on to Delhi. I found it awe-inspiring to see thousands of people gathering each evening to hear the story of Jesus. There were so many open hearts and so many responding to the message of God's love for a broken world.

In Jalandhar I purchased a second-class train ticket and boarded what has been described as a moving Indian bazaar. The train was like a festival on wheels. The whole length of the carriage was filled to capacity with men, women and children. There was so much noise and vibrancy as people talked together and shared food. At each station, people would climb on board selling food or novelty items. The hot-tea sellers would arrive shouting out their loud cry of '*chai, chai, garam chai*' and we would order hot, sweet *chai* served in small clay cups. Then, for those who were hungry, the samosa *wallah* (person) made his way through the crowd selling hot, spicy samosas served in bowls made of dried leaves, the aroma of the samosas filling the air. At other times, the sound of a beautiful, soulful, rhythmic voice would break into the usual noise made by the chattering crowd as a singer would come to entertain. Making his way along the carriage he might be singing of love or the pain of a life of struggle. A few coins placed into his hand would send him on his way. These and many others would join us along the incredible journey of life that is the Indian train.

The train chugged its way across the great Indian plains. Leaving the vast wheat fields of the Punjab, we entered a more desert-like terrain as we approached Delhi. There seemed to be no end to the land, which stretched out in every direction. It seemed to go on forever. Leaving the many villages and fields, we headed into the suburbs of that great city, which is filled with history and culture. Now there was noise, bustle and excitement as we neared New Delhi train station and where we finally came to a halt. As I stepped off the train, I was taken aback by the never-ending crowds of people moving in every direction. Whole families and individuals were on the move amidst the noise and chaos, with *coolies* (labourers) in their red *kurta* shirts, carrying great loads on their heads.

I made my way through the crowds and walked out of the station. Here were streets filled with people and a constant stream of activity. Everywhere there was noise and shouting, and all around was the aroma of street food and spices mingled with the fragrant smell of burning incense. As I stood there trying to take all of this in, I was instantly impacted with a gigantic, colourful, shimmering billboard towering above me, which was advertising the latest Bollywood movie.

I got into an auto rickshaw and headed for the address that I'd been given for Dilaram House. Arriving, I stepped out of the vehicle and, taking some money from the few rupees I had left, paid the driver. As he drove away, I looked at my hands. In one, I held a crumpled piece of paper on which was scribbled the address; in the other, I had my remaining Indian rupees. The money God had provided in Amsterdam was the amount I'd needed from beginning to end. It also struck me that I was beginning my new life in India with nothing more than an address and a handful of rupees. Years later, I would look back on that day and count the many blessings of God's provision over the years.

I entered the door of the large house and was met by an Australian lady who was a part of the Dilaram team. Her first words to me were, 'You're short.' I said, 'I'm what?' She said, 'Shorter than I thought.' She went on to say that because I had such a large amount of mail waiting for me, she thought I would be extremely tall. I found it quite humorous and never could quite make the connection. It was great to finally be here, and I immediately felt a part of all that was happening. There were about twenty to thirty people living, community-style, in the building. Some were staff, some were new Christians and some were seekers.

India is famous for its ashrams, and some travellers who were spiritual seekers would stay in an ashram for a period of time on their spiritual search. Basically, an ashram is a religious community which is dedicated to spiritual instruction, meditation and prayer. They are more common within the Hindu culture. Ashrams had a great appeal to hippies and other world travellers who were searching for spiritual meaning or direction and were looking for somewhere to search at their own pace and without pressure. Dilaram offered that in a Christian context.

As Dilaram was reaching out to the hippy community, which included literally thousands of people across India at that time, the ministry operated in a way that was close to the ashram system. People could come and visit, or live with us, if they wanted to know more about Jesus or the Christian faith. The ministry was based in a building that had been built as a guest house and it had plenty of rooms with attached bathrooms, and an outlying building in the small compound. It was situated in an area which, at that time, was on the outskirts of the city. Each morning we would gather for prayer, and at various times through the week we would go on outreach. This was usually to Paharganj, an inner-city area populated by hippy travellers. On a few occasions I visited Delhi's famous Tihar Jail, where I met with foreign travellers who had been sentenced to imprisonment for drug trafficking or some other crime. We would connect with people travelling through Delhi, and many became Christians during that time.

We had arrived in India at the beginning of the hot season, when temperatures rise dramatically, so things slowed down somewhat, especially through the hottest period during the afternoons. Some days I would walk out of the house and make my way towards an open area of desert wilderness at the edge of our housing colony. I enjoyed the wide, open space of the desert, which spread out in every direction. The sunsets would be magnificent as the sun descended beyond the horizon in a great ball of red flame. Because the house was always full of people, I loved going there to pray and to be alone with God.

I loved India from the day I arrived, and what was new to me soon became normal to my everyday life. Unlike some people,

I didn't experience any kind of culture shock at all and, as time went on, I became one with everything around me. I grew to love the great loudness of colour, music, sounds and noise mixed with the smells and aromas of food, incense and spices. I loved the crowds and warmth and passion of the people, and I loved living in a nation filled with adventure and drama expressed through the exuberant, joyful celebration of life which is India. Whether it was New Delhi's modern Connaught Place with its upmarket shopping, or Janpath where we could bargain for trinkets and souvenirs, or the myriad of crowded, twisting, narrow lanes in the densely packed bazaars of Old Delhi, I loved it all.

I had been in Delhi for five months. In the outbuilding at the back of the house, there were steps that led up to a cemented flat roof. It was now September, and the climate was beginning to cool slightly from the oppressive heat of summer. Along with the wide-open space of the nearby desert, this was my favourite place of solitude. Sometimes early morning, or at other times late afternoon, I would climb the steps to the roof to be alone and pray and find silence. This was one of those times when I was alone. There was a warm, gentle breeze blowing in from the desert as I sat on the low wall at the edge of the rooftop. The monsoon season had come to an end and the air felt dry. As I looked out across the surrounding houses, I thought about my time in Delhi, and I thanked God for the way he had led me over the years. I had such a peace and contentment in my heart and thought of how blessed I was to be able to serve God in such an amazing place. Then, in that moment of silent solitude, these words, gentle but powerful, came to my heart: 'You will be leaving India.'

11

The Valley of the Lotus

I came down the steps from the rooftop, and as I approached the side of the house, Dave, who led the community with his wife, Angie, came towards me. In his hand he held a letter, which had just come in the post. 'Geoff,' he said. 'I was just on my way to find you.' I looked at him and waited to hear what he had to say next. He told me that he had just received a letter from the Dilaram community in Kathmandu, Nepal requesting that they send someone to help them with their ministry in that city. Apparently, they needed another male member to help. Dave continued speaking: 'I wanted to ask you if you'd be willing to go.' I smiled and told him what I had felt God say just a few moments previously. We agreed that I was the one to go.

Most Western travellers going from Delhi to Kathmandu would take the overland route, which meant taking a train to the Nepal border and from there travelling by bus to Kathmandu. This would involve a journey of eight hours along winding roads through the mountains. Being the end of the monsoon season, we knew that sections of the mountain roads would have experienced landslides caused by the heavy rains, so we decided I should fly for part of the journey.

Within a few days I boarded a train bound for the city of Patna from where I would fly north, over the border, to Kathmandu.

As the train made its way out of the station, we travelled through Delhi until we left the great urban sprawl behind us and moved into open countryside. Again, I was amazed at the vastness of this great land. I arrived early the next morning at Patna train station and from there took one of the many cycle rickshaws to the small airport. I felt sad to be leaving India but excited at the same time as I anticipated what lay ahead.

Clearing immigration, I boarded the aircraft and, with a great heave, the plane lifted itself from the runway, and we were on our way. The sky was clear blue with brilliant sunshine, which gave me a great view of the plains below. This was North India where the Gangetic Plains stretch out for miles in every direction, and thousands of villages are scattered across the land. We flew over the great river Ganges as it flowed through the terrain to the end of its journey in the Bay of Bengal, its waters shimmering in the reflection of the sun. Looking from the window, I saw what looked like an enormous patchwork quilt made of fabrics of earthy colours. Small clusters of green appeared in various places around closely knit village houses nestled among clumps of trees.

As we continued, we reached the Himalayan foothills. Now the earthy colours of brown, beige and russet changed colour as we soared high above forest-covered hills. Fed by the recent monsoon rains, the hills and distant mountains had become a rich green. Then suddenly, the majestic snow-covered mountains of the Himalayas were before us. Here was the roof of the world. Spread out like a great arc across the horizon, and with the snows reflecting the brilliance of the sun, the mountains appeared like a shimmering diamond-filled tiara placed by God upon the planet Earth. It was breathtaking.

We now began our descent into the Kathmandu Valley, and as the plane moved closer to the land, it made its way across smaller mountains and hills as we approached the city. Small houses of rustic design were nestled into man-made terraces which were carved into the mountainsides. Water-filled terraces shimmered brilliantly as the sun reflected upon their emerald hue of newly planted rice, and streams and rivers shone silver. Turning towards the airport, the plane descended until the wheels touched the tarmac of the small runway and we came to a halt. Leaving the airport, I climbed into an auto rickshaw and made my way to the Dilaram community.

We continued along the road, which skirted the edge of the city, and followed its ascent until we came to Sanepa, the area where Dilaram House was situated. Established at a higher level, a few miles from the city, Sanepa had more of a semi-rural feel rather than that of city suburbs. Once an open area of farmland, it now contained houses that had been built around the mission hospital, which was housed in an old palace. Although there had been a small increase in house building in the area over recent years, they were very few, and well spaced out. The whole area had an open, peaceful feel, which disconnected it from the hustle and bustle of the city below. Having said that, Kathmandu in no way felt like the more heavily populated mega cities of India and other parts of Asia.

The house was in a perfect place for the ministry in which we were involved, as we could bring people out of the city and into this quiet locality where there was little distraction. From the rooftop of the house, one could look in every direction and see the most amazing scenery. From one side, we could look out across an extended valley, which stretched out before us until it touched the surrounding hills and mountains. The fields across the valley were filled with emerald-green shoots of rice fed by flowing water from mountain streams. During the day, the whole area glistened in the sun as women in their large, round, woven rattan hats would sing, chatter and laugh before the sun would finally begin to set and they would make their way home.

Looking in the other direction, we would see the old city spread out below us. This was before the population increase and expanding urbanisation that we see in Kathmandu today. From here, the city, with its ancient streets, tightly packed houses and tall pagoda-like temples stretched out across the valley until it reached the nearby mountains, which ascended in loftiness until they touched the sky. All seemed to exist in a period beyond time, taking us back to a bygone age untouched by the modern world. As a backdrop to this age-old city was the great panorama of the mighty Himalayas, enveloped in snow and exciting the imagination with wonder, its ancient passes carrying the legends of those who had travelled their treacherous depths. And then, behind the lofty peaks lay the dark and mysterious land of ancient Tibet. From its hilltop stronghold at the edge of the city, the eyes of the large, imposing Swayambhunath temple kept watch over the valley. As the sun would set each evening, the white snow-covered mountains would be set ablaze with a great hue of pink, purple and crimson as God turned on his extravagant light show declaring the majesty of his creation.

The nation of Nepal is filled with myths and legends and one holds that the Kathmandu Valley was once an expansive lake upon which grew a very large and beautiful lotus flower, thus the legend of the Valley of the Lotus. One day, it is said, one of the gods descended upon the earth, and with one mighty swoop of his sword, he split the mountains and drained the valley, thus making a way for the waters to flow out through the smaller mountains and hills below. No one is sure whether the valley ever contained a large lake, but we do know that the city has existed since around 300bc and was a major trade route between South and Central Asia.

Large-scale migrations have occurred over the centuries bringing movements of tribes and castes into Nepal. While some have come from India in the south, others have migrated from Tibet in the north. This has brought about the mixture of diverse ethnic groups, religions, cultures, customs, cuisine and languages that make up the unique nation of Nepal. Although Nepal is officially the world's only Hindu kingdom, it is also strongly influenced by Buddhism. While I lived there, it was said that Kathmandu had more than 27,000 shrines dedicated to gods and deities, making that number greater than houses that existed in the city. In 1769, King Prithvi Narayan Shah conquered the valley and sealed off Nepal to the outside world. This continued until 1950 when a revolution took place and brought in the monarchy, which existed during the time I lived in Kathmandu. The king was said to be an incarnation of one of the gods.

My time was soon taken up with the various ministries connected to Dilaram as we reached out to Western travellers arriving in the city. Several afternoons each week, our small team would make its way, on foot, into the city, which was always an interesting adventure. I still vividly remember my walks on that short but exciting journey which, in time, became so familiar to me.

Leaving the house, we would walk across the garden, and after passing under the arch of strongly fragranced jasmine blossom that swept above the gate, we would merge onto the street. Following the road towards the city, we would turn off onto a small dirt path, which took us into an area of open space. Here we would pass the ancient tree that had a seat made of old bricks and cement around its base where old men would gather to sit and tell their tales. Maybe they would talk about the old days, but to me, looking at the scene, which spread out across the fields and terraces towards the ancient city, it was still the old days, as nothing seemed to have changed for centuries. Following the dirt path across rice fields, we would come to the rickety old walking bridge that crossed the Bagmati River. To the right of us was a scene out of antiquity as ageless, crumbling temples touched the river's edge. This was the funeral Ghat where the deceased were cremated on great piles of wood as priests made prayers and ablutions in the hope that the soul who had passed would be reborn into a better life. Plumes of smoke rose from the funeral pyre mingling with the chant of ancient Sanskrit prayers.

After crossing the bridge, we would enter the old city. Here ancient houses lined the narrow street, their low doors and small windows made of intricately crafted wood, which had been artistically and creatively carved by generations of craftsmen. As we walked, the gentle strain of Eastern music and the scent of fragrant incense would drift from behind the latticework of darkened windows, and we would head into the bazaar. As the houses merged into the noisy, bustling market, we would catch the aroma of spices and freshly cooked food. We'd pass the dentist with his primitive equipment, then the barber giving a haircut or head massage, and the butcher with his goats' heads hanging from hooks on the outside wall. Now the sweet shops and the sari shops and the sellers of bangles and glass-beaded necklaces worn by married women. In each place, people would be haggling over the price of goods in an effort to get the best bargain. Finally, we would turn the corner at the ancient temples and, crossing Durbar Square with its old royal palace and the Temple of the Living Goddess, reach our destination of Freak Street.

Freak Street, which was located in the Basantapur area of the old city, was a name given to a street that was populated with seasoned hippies and new arrivals. This was the centre of the Kathmandu hippy scene where, until shortly before my arrival, hashish and marijuana was legally sold openly in the shops, restaurants and hotels. Small, low-budget hotels in tiny Nepalese buildings lined both sides of the street, where narrow staircases led to equally small, darkened rooms. The hotels along the street were broken by tightly packed restaurants serving low-cost Western-style food and trinket shops selling brass idols, silver jewellery, souvenirs and other items of interest to the traveller who was preparing to return home. Drugs and spirituality were two things that drew people to the Freak Street area. This was where some had their heads messed up from too many magic mushrooms or too much hashish, while others became disillusioned in their spiritual search.

It was to these people that we reached out. Some of them, because of drug-related problems, were desperate for help. Others ended up ill, and would sometimes be sent to us from the mission hospital and would stay with us as we helped nurse them back to health. Through this time people from all kinds of backgrounds came to visit or stay with us, and it was our greatest joy to see people give their lives to Christ and become his followers. To those who were sick, he became their healer, to those who were messed up from drugs, he became their liberator, and to those who were spiritually searching, he became the end of their search. Surrendering to him, each one would find peace. The dark side of the area surrounding Freak Street was the underground business that went on behind the scenes, which involved drug trafficking, prostitution and other areas of criminal activity.

The ministry of Dilaram existed with a calling to reach out to travellers along the then existing hippy trail rather than local people. Although we lived in Nepal, appreciated the culture and mingled with local people, we pretty much remained within a community of world travellers and foreign missionaries. However, as I visited Basantapur each week, I began to get to know some of the local people who were living and working in that area. As a result, I began to get an increasing burden to reach out to local Nepalese people, whom I was now meeting on an almost daily basis, with the good news of Jesus.

I knew by now that, out of a population of 16 million people, there were only a very small handful of indigenous Christian believers in Nepal. There were a few churches, but these were, almost totally, made up of foreigners who were living and working in Nepal. This included the church we attended on Sundays, which met in an international school. Apart from the small number of believers, the whole nation of Nepal was totally unreached with the gospel. Living in remote, difficult-to-access mountain villages, millions of people had never heard the name of Jesus and didn't know Christianity existed. This began to grow in me day and night and became a priority in my times of prayer.

Following my pattern from Delhi, it became a practice on some evenings, after dinner, to climb the steps onto the rooftop where I would spend time in prayer before the sun set beyond the mountains and darkness descended over the city. Inspired by the majestic mountains, I would worship God and be in awe of his creation. A verse from the Bible which came alive to me at that time was Psalm 121:1–2 which says, 'I lift up my eyes to the mountains – where does my help come from? My help comes from the LORD, the Maker of heaven and earth.'

One evening, as I looked out toward the lofty Himalayan peaks, I felt the Holy Spirit begin to move on my heart. Gazing into the distance, I saw range after range of mountains rising from the valley and ascending until, stretched in a great panoramic view from the west to the east, snow-covered summits touched the heavens. I thought about the hundreds of valleys, with their thousands of villages containing millions of people scattered across the land; many of them accessible only by long tracks that ran along ancient foot-worn mountain trails, some of which could only be reached after weeks of walking.

As I prayed, in my spirit, I saw valley after valley and village after village filled with people whom God loved and wanted to reach. Then, God began to give me a vision of valleys filled with the glory of God and people worshipping Jesus across the length and breadth of the land. I felt God say that the day would come when every valley in that unreached land would resound with the sound of people singing God's praises as they worshipped him. I began to pray, 'Lord, please send people to reach these precious souls who so desperately need you. You have promised to send workers into your harvest field in answer to our prayers. Please send workers until all hear your message of love and grace.'

As my heart cried out to God, it never dawned on me that I should offer myself to go. I was working with Dilaram, which focused on Kathmandu hippies, so believed the work among local Nepalese people was someone else's call. I continued asking God to raise others up to go. I was somewhat like the wonderful missionary Gladys Aylward who had a burden for China and while in England prayed that God would send her brother. She didn't think she would qualify to go. She eventually went to China and did a great work for God in that nation. As I sat, looking out towards the mountains, I heard the quiet voice of God speak to my heart: 'I want *you* to go.'

12

Into the Mountains

Amos 9:13 says, '"The days are coming," declares the LORD, "when the reaper will be overtaken by the ploughman and the planter by the one treading grapes. New wine will drip from the mountains and flow from all the hills"'. Verses like this would encourage me as I prayed. I would pray into verses like this one in Amos declaring that one day the new wine of God's Spirit would flow through the mountains, hills and valleys of Nepal resulting in praise and glory to Jesus in every place across the land.

I began to notice other verses in the Bible that mention mountains. Isaiah 49:13 says, 'Shout for joy, you heavens; rejoice, you earth; burst into song, you mountains! For the LORD comforts his people and will have compassion on his afflicted ones.' Being one of the poorest countries in the world, I knew that Nepal was filled with people who suffered every day in an effort to just survive. All across the mountains people survived on the very little they could grow on small patches of land. Millions were cut off from the modern world, living in areas where there was no education or medical facilities. I prayed that God would have compassion on the afflicted across the nation. Isaiah 52:7 says, 'How beautiful on the mountains are the feet of those who bring good news, who proclaim peace, who bring good tidings, who proclaim salvation, who say to Zion, "Your God reigns!"' These and other verses gave great encouragement as I continued to pray.

I didn't say anything to anyone else at that time about how I was feeling but kept it all in my heart. I continued to pray until a few days later when Steve, who led the Dilaram community with his wife, Kathy, asked me when I had last taken a holiday. I couldn't think when I'd ever really taken a break. He continued, 'Why don't you take a week off? We're not so busy right now and this would be a good time to go.'

The timing seemed perfect, and I knew exactly what I had to do. I would head into the mountains. Trekking was one of the main activities attracting people to Nepal, and there were many trails carved out across the mountains. These treks could last anywhere from a few days to a few weeks. I checked out some options and worked out a trek that would last one week. This would fit in with the time I had to take a break. I would have loved to have had someone to travel with, but as no one was able to go, I decided that I would go alone. My main purpose was to reach people on mountain trails and in villages with the good news of Jesus and, where possible, introduce them to him.

One problem that I faced was that I could not speak Nepali, the main language of Nepal, so I would not be able to communicate with people verbally. As I prayed, I thought of the next best thing I could use, which was literature. At that time, although the Bible was available in the Nepali language, there were no gospel tracts or other literature that clearly explained the gospel message. After making some enquiries, I was able to get hold of some booklets of the Gospel of John in Nepali.

As Christianity was almost non-existent, and Nepal being officially a Hindu kingdom, I was warned by some friends about the existing laws before I left. Conversion to Christianity was strictly prohibited, resulting in arrest and criminal punishment. According to the legal system, punishment for conversion to Christianity was one year of imprisonment for the convert, three years imprisonment for a person who converted another to Christianity, and six years imprisonment for a person who baptised someone into the Christian faith. This was something I took very seriously, and I gave it great thought and prayer. However, as I knew that God was leading me, I was determined to follow him whatever the consequences. People needed to hear the life-changing message of Jesus and I had said 'yes' to God.

I discovered that there had often been opposition to conversion in Nepal over the previous centuries. I learned that Italian Capuchin priests, serving the Roman Catholic Church, had entered Nepal and visited Kathmandu while on their way to Tibet. Other priests followed and lived in the city and at one time, three large crosses were placed upon the hills surrounding the Kathmandu Valley. However, none of the priests had been able to establish anything long-term because of opposition.

I read that a few Indian Christians were able to cross the border into Nepal, including the great Indian preacher and mystic, Sadhu Sundar Singh. Following his conversion to Christianity, this man of prayer and faith travelled the Himalayan paths of Nepal, India and Tibet, living simply and sharing the good news of Jesus with all who would listen. He made many attempts to preach in Nepal, but each time he was met with rejection and persecution. One time he was badly beaten and securely fastened in stocks while leeches were thrown onto his body, yet he continued preaching. Around the same time missionaries, who had a burden for the Nepalese people, had set up well-established mission stations along the Indian side of the border where they would pray for Nepal and minister to those who crossed into India.

The day came for me to begin my trip, and I packed as many small books of the Gospel of John as I could physically carry into my backpack and placed it over my shoulders. I had learned a few phrases of Nepali that would help me along the way. I could ask people if they would like a book, tell them it was God's book, and ask if there was somewhere I could spend the night. I felt that, because I didn't speak the language, I may not be able to accomplish as much as I would have liked, but at least I could place the written words of Jesus into people's hands and trust God with the outcome.

The Bible tells the story of a small boy who only had a few loaves of bread and some fish when thousands needed feeding. It seemed inadequate for the need but, as he placed what he had into the hands of Jesus, a miracle occurred (John 6:1–13). Sometimes we don't feel that we have much to offer God, or we may feel inadequate for the task, but if we just place what we have into his hands he can multiply what we give him and use us to bless others while working miracles through our lives.

Climbing into the bus, I headed out of the city. I travelled for a few hours until I reached the village from where I would begin my trek through the mountains. As I stepped out onto the road, the bus pulled away and continued its own journey north toward the Tibetan border. I made my way along a village street and into the open countryside. The sun was warm and the sky a radiant blue as I made my way along the valley. I followed a path along the side of a river, the sound of its crystal-clear waters, cascading over rocks and boulders, filling the air. After spending so much time in the city, the silence was so noticeable and the air was so clear and pure. I continued along the valley until the path I was on began its ascent into the surrounding mountains. I began to climb, placing my feet firmly upon the ancient, stony path, which was well-worn from the footsteps of those who had trodden upon it for years, and maybe even centuries, before. As I travelled along the trail, people would occasionally come towards me from the opposite direction, and I would offer them one of God's books.

By now it was late afternoon, and as I walked along the path, I saw a Western guy ahead of me making his way up the trail. He looked as though he was struggling to make the climb. I eventually caught up with him, and we introduced ourselves. He was from New York and said that a number of his friends had been trekking in Nepal, so he decided to try it himself. He went on to say that he hadn't realised how out of shape he was. Following the map I had brought with me, I had worked out where I would stay each night along the trail. We continued along the path together until we reached a small cluster of houses where I had planned to spend the night.

Built into the side of the mountain, each house was simple in its structure and consisted of two rooms. The upstairs room housed the whole family where they lived, slept and cooked, and the room on ground level was where they kept their animals through the night. This was the first time I had stayed with local people, and I enjoyed my time trying to communicate, using sign language, with the family who were our hosts. This brought lots of laughter on both sides, and I felt very much at home. Our room for the night was on the ground floor where, after a gigantic serving of rice, lentil soup (*dal*) and vegetable curry, we settled into the straw which was to be our bed for the night. In one corner of the room, a goat was tethered to a post, and after a fitful night's sleep, when I was bitten by bugs living in the straw and had to wrestle with a hen who wanted to share my bed space, we were ready for a new day. After a breakfast of more rice, *dal* and vegetable curry, we went on our way.

As a part of our trek was along the same path, I decided to travel with the guy from New York until we would go in different directions the next day. My concern was that I wanted to give out the literature I had brought with me, which would have been difficult if I was with him. I'm pretty sure he wouldn't have approved of what I was doing, and at the same time, I didn't want to get him into any kind of trouble for my giving out Christian literature. This was resolved by him having to stop at short distances to rest when I would go on a little way ahead, so that I was free to give out the gospels I was carrying.

The daily walk was timed so that each evening, before sunset, we would reach a particular village that would give us a place to sleep and provide food. Because the guy I was travelling with was going so slowly, I was concerned that we wouldn't make it to the next village before sunset. Failure to reach the place where we would spend the night would mean that we would get trapped somewhere out in the mountains overnight. As we journeyed on, I became more certain that we were not going to make it to our destination for that evening. My thoughts proved true.

A section of the route we were on connected with a river. This meant that we had to walk along the riverbed until it reconnected with the trail. The sun was already beginning to set before we got to the river, and I was concerned that darkness would overtake us. To reach the river, we had to descend down the mountain and into a valley. For every step we took downwards into the valley, the sun made its own descent behind the mountains above us, and we quickly became enveloped in darkness. Because I'd carefully studied a map before I left Kathmandu and knew that I would easily get to where I needed to stay each evening, I had not brought a flashlight with me. This meant we would not be able to see the way.

By the time we got to the river, we were in total darkness. Because we were at a high altitude, there was a sudden drop in temperature. I knew that it was too cold to sleep outside. We had to go forward. Feeling our way along the river's edge, we stumbled over boulders and rocks as we waded through the water. At one place the sides of the river turned into sheer, vertical cliffs of rock rising above us so that we were locked in from both sides. We were now cold, wet and exhausted, and I prayed that God would help us find our way forward and bring us to a place where we could safely spend the night. We continued until, with a great sense of relief and gratitude to God, I saw a faint, flicker of light in the far distance.

Finding new strength, we made our way onward until we came to a small bamboo shelter built into a clearing at the foot of the mountain. From a gentle glow of light emanating from the structure, I saw a water buffalo tethered to a post outside, and an old man sitting inside warming his hands against an open fire stoked with pieces of wood. He initially looked startled at the sight of two Westerners rising from the riverbed. Through gestures and actions, we tried as best we could to explain what had happened, and understanding our situation, he invited us to spend the night in his shelter.

Although our accommodation was a very primitive structure with a dried dirt floor, we were very grateful, and I thanked God for his provision. By now we were hungry but saw no sign of food. That was soon remedied, however, as we heard a sound coming from the narrow trail on the mountain behind us. Entering the shelter, a young boy exchanged some words with the old man and, lifting up the front of his hat, pulled out a fish. This was cooked with rice, and we all had dinner. This definitely was not 5-star accommodation, but to me that night, it was a blessing sent by God.

13

A Narrow Escape and a New Direction

We slept that night and early next morning continued our journey until we got to the next village, and then went in different directions. I continued on my own, climbing mountain trails that at times dipped into hidden valleys. At one point, I came down the path and saw the back of a large stone-built house ahead of me, which was constructed in the same style as other houses in the area. Sitting cross-legged on some grass just a short distance from the front of the house were a group of men playing a card game.

As I approached, they looked in my direction and stopped what they were doing. I thought this would be a good opportunity to give them some of the literature I was carrying, so moved towards them. One of the men looked like the leader of the group, and as I approached, looking at him, I asked them if they would like some books. The leader of the group asked me what kind of books. I replied that they were God's books. I passed one to him and, taking it in his hand, he opened it and began to study its contents. By now I sensed that something wasn't right and could feel a slight tension. He looked at the other men and then looked at me, studying my face. When, once again, he looked into the pages of the book I turned to look at the front of the large house which was behind me. On the front of the building, above the door, was a large painted sign. Being in the local written script, I couldn't read the writing but I did recognise it from similar signs I had seen in Kathmandu. I now realised that I was in front of the local police station for that area and that these men were the local police. At this point, the guy who was holding the book, and obviously the man in charge, looked at me again and slowly nodded his head with a serious look on his face.

Inside, I prayed, asking God what I should do. Knowing what I'd been told about the law, I knew that there was a possibility that this may not end well. I actually thought of quickly moving on, but in the end, I knew that all I could do was trust God with the outcome, so I just stood there and silently prayed. Sometimes we find ourselves in situations that are out of our control, and this was one of them. When there is nothing we can do about a situation we find ourselves in, we can trust God to work things out on our behalf, and this is what I decided to do. While I waited to see what was going to happen, the guy reading the Gospel of John asked me to give him more books. I passed more to him, and with a smile on his face, he handed one to each of the other men and thanked me. I was so relieved when each of them expressed their gratitude and sent me on my way. All the way down the trail I thanked God for keeping me safe and prayed that he would use the literature I had given to bring the abundant life that Jesus promised to each of these men and their families.

I continued along the trail, still giving out the literature I was carrying, until I came to the village where I would spend the night. By now I was thankful that my backpack was a lot lighter than when I'd started the journey, and I had very few gospels left. On entering the village, I saw that it was bigger, and slightly more developed, than the other villages I had travelled through, which were really only small hamlets. It was a beautiful sunny day as I walked along the wide, cobbled path. Houses ran along both sides of the path, and in the centre of the village were several shops selling basic everyday goods that supplied the needs of the people in the village and those who lived in the surrounding mountains. In the centre was a *chai* shop, which sold tea and a few small dishes of freshly cooked food items.

This was a stopping-off place for those who were travelling up and down the mountain trail. The *chai* shop's soot-blackened kettle, filled with hot, sweet, milky tea, sat in pride of place on the open wood-stoked fire, always ready to refresh the weary traveller. Being on a main route, there was always a flow of people pausing to drink tea and catch up with whatever news had drifted up, or down, the mountains. All of the houses had flowering plants placed in containers outside their windows giving the whole place a picturesque, alpine look. In its simplicity, it held a certain charm. Asking around, I found a room in one of the houses, which was situated directly above the bazaar. This was perfect for me, as I could look down from my window onto the constant flow of Nepalese mountain-village life below. The room was simple but clean and comfortable, and I made myself at home. It actually had a bed, a real bed, and although it had a mattress stuffed with straw, it was a great luxury after the other places in which I'd slept.

The next day, around mid-morning, I went down to the *chai* shop to drink tea and try to get to know some of the people. As I sat in the morning sun, I was approached from one of the houses by a young Nepalese man, who came over to me and introduced himself in English. I was overjoyed to be able to finally communicate with someone, and we immediately struck up a flowing conversation. He had been educated in Kathmandu, and on completing his education, his work in forestry had placed him in this area. We talked for a while and, at one point in the conversation, I told him that I was a Christian. 'You are a Christian,' he said excitedly. 'I'm also a Christian.' He went on to say that before he was sent to this village, he had met some Christians and had given his life to Christ. With little knowledge of what it meant to live out the Christian life, and having no Bible, he had been praying that God would send another Christian who would be able to spend some time with him.

I almost felt that I'd made this trip just for him. We spent a wonderful two days together, talking and praying. It was a special time, and I promised to keep in touch after I had left. It reminded me of how so often God wants us to be the answer to the prayers of another person. I could have actually taken another route, but God directed me to the exact place where this guy, who was precious to God, had been praying for another Christian to come along with whom he could spend time.

My journey had now come to an end, and I knew that my next walk along the long, verdant valley would take me to the main road from where I would get on a bus which would take me back to the city. As I walked along the valley, with mountains rising above me on either side, I inhaled the pure mountain air and felt the sun's rays on my face. I listened to the sounds all around me, the shouts and voices from distant homes and mountain terraces, the rippling of the river's water flowing over the rocks, the song of birds and the sound of the breeze blowing through the trees. I took it all in and knew something had happened in my heart. I was returning a different person with a new and different call upon my life. While I had enjoyed reaching out to world travellers through the ministry of Dilaram, I knew now that God was changing the direction of my life and that my heart was being turned towards reaching the people of Nepal. I didn't know what the next step would be but, once again, I trusted God to lead me and work it all out. I didn't know it at the time, but major change would come sooner than I had thought.

Returning to Kathmandu, I resumed my work with the Dilaram community and continued to wait on God for his direction and timing on what I should do next. I have always found it important to wait on God for his timing in any plan of direction he has placed upon my heart. It's so easy to get excited about something God has called us to do and then run off ahead of him. His time is always the right time. I also knew that there were several things I needed to put in place, and some things to consider, before I made the next move.

First of all, there was the situation with Dilaram, a ministry which was called to work with world travellers. Because of this, and because of the stringent laws on people changing religion in Nepal, Dilaram ministry had restricted itself to only working with foreign hippy travellers, not with local people. The reason for this was because the whole ministry could be closed down if they started reaching out to local people, and this would jeopardise what they believed to be their main call from God. I knew that if I began to reach out to Nepalese people, I would have to separate from Dilaram, although we would always remain friends. That would add a second consideration, which was that although Dilaram did not pay a salary, they did cover my accommodation and food. I had absolutely no financial support from any source, and because I still felt that I should not make my needs known, I would have to trust God completely.

Other things I needed to consider were that I could not speak the Nepali language and basically didn't know what I should even do next. I made the decision I had made many times before, and that was to trust God, knowing that if he was the one who was calling me, he would have a plan. I also knew that if he was asking me to do something for him, then he would provide. Once again, I was reminded of verses in the Bible where God has promised to provide our needs. I held on to these verses, believing that God would make a way and provide all that I needed when the time came to move on.

I continued going to Freak Street several afternoons each week where we continued to reach out to world travellers; however, this time it was different for me personally. As I had a growing burden to reach local people, I found myself drawn increasingly to those living and working in that area of the city. These included Nepalese restaurant and hotel owners and their staff as well as Nepalese people who would generally just hang out in the neighbourhood. Some of these would include small-time drug dealers who were operating in Basantapur and supplying people with hashish and other drugs. Obviously, the constant flow of hippy travellers kept them in business and provided for their livelihood. Added to this was the business of stolen passports and traveller's cheques as well as drug smuggling and prostitution.

It was becoming clear to me that this was the area in which I should live, and these were the people I should reach out to with the life-changing message of Jesus. I felt that because I couldn't speak the local language, it would be a great help if I had a Nepalese Christian join me. So I began to pray, asking God to provide someone who would also be called to work with me in reaching people in that area of Kathmandu I had become so familiar with. I left my request with God, believing that he would provide a strong, mature Christian, maybe someone who had been a Christian for many years and who knew the Bible really well. Maybe even someone from a Bible college. However, God had other plans.

One afternoon I was walking along Freak Street. Noise and chatter were going on all around me, and the usual colourful hippy travellers were either walking around outside or in shops buying goods and trinkets. Familiar late sixties and early seventies hippy music poured out of open restaurant doors. As I made my way down the street, I noticed a young, local guy standing outside the doorway of one of the restaurants. Looking at him, I guessed that he either managed the restaurant or ran it as his own business. I'd never been in that particular restaurant, so I'd never actually met him, nor had I seen him, before. When I went home that evening, I kept thinking about him and felt the Holy Spirit urging me to pray that he would come to know Jesus. This continued and on a couple of occasions over the following days I tried to talk to him when I saw him outside the restaurant. Each time I tried to talk to him he would be distracted by something, or someone, so we never really got a chance to engage in any kind of lengthy conversation. The next several times I visited Freak Street, I looked for him but couldn't find him anywhere on the street, or at the restaurant, but kept praying for him.

At this time a Bible teacher came from England and was conducting several days of Bible studies in the home of some foreign missionaries. Those of us living in the Dilaram community had been invited to attend and went for the morning session. Entering the compound, we walked across the garden towards the building and entered the front room of the house, which was filled with people. To my amazement, when I looked across the room, I saw the guy from the restaurant, whom I'd been praying for, sitting in the corner. The meeting began and when it concluded I walked over to meet him. He recognised me from Freak Street, introduced himself as Claude, and began to tell his story. He had been away from the restaurant for the past couple of weeks. One day, he had what could only be explained as an encounter with Jesus. He sensed God's presence fill the room where he was staying, and he kept thinking of something his grandmother, who had lived in India, told him many years ago about Jesus. As he began to think deeply about what she had said, he started to pray, and alone in the room surrendered his life to Christ.

On his return he made some enquiries and was directed towards an Indian missionary who helped him and had brought him to the Bible study group we were in today. I asked him what his plans were. 'Above all else,' he said, 'I want to go back into the Basantapur area and reach the people living and working there with the good news of Jesus. I want to tell them what Jesus has done for me and how he has changed my life.' I shared with him what God had been saying to me and told him of my desire to reach the same people, in the same area, with the gospel. I went on to say that I had been praying for someone to join me in the task and, although he had only been a Christian for a matter of days, he became the perfect person. He knew the area really well, he knew many of the local people, he knew all the ins and outs of what was going on both on the surface as well as behind the scenes, and he spoke the language. That day a team was born.

We immediately became friends and began to meet together to pray, plan and seek God for the way forward. I had shared my plans with the rest of the team in the Dilaram community, and they also joined with me in prayer. It was such a blessing to have their prayer support, wisdom and insight as I was preparing for what God had next. As Claude and I met together, we began to pray that God would provide either an apartment or a small house in the heart of Basantapur. We would use this as a base, and it would be an open house for all who wanted to come. We would open it up as a place where all were welcome to visit and talk over tea or coffee, and we would share our faith. We prayed that God would use us to bring people to Jesus.

Whenever we talked and prayed about all of this, we would often laugh at the fact that neither of us had enough money to rent a room and certainly not a house or apartment. Claude had decided to leave the restaurant where he worked, and like the disciples of old, we would work for God and trust him to provide our needs. I had no doubt that the God who had faithfully led me this far would guide me the rest of the way. When we walk with God, we don't always know where the next step will take us, and the one I was now about to take would be one of the most scary, risk-taking steps of faith I had taken so far, where I had nothing and no one but God to rely on. And in that place of faith, some amazing things were about to happen.

14

Next Door to a Goddess

In Nepal, many gods and goddesses are worshipped and revered, but one stands out as unique to this nation, and that is
the Living Goddess. Considered an embodiment of the fero-
cious goddess Taleju, the Living Goddess, or Kumari as she is
also known, is both feared and worshipped by all. The word
'Kumari' means 'young girl' or 'virgin'. Her temple is situated in
the heart of Durbar Square, just a short walk from Freak Street.

The process of her selection has always been shrouded in
mystery and, by order of the priests, kept secret in this age-old
tradition, which apparently has existed for several hundred
years. However, I was told that through time, tales of what
takes place have become known until, like pieces of a jigsaw
puzzle, the whole process has come together and become common knowledge in Nepal.

In seeking to discover more, I was told that the rituals involved are very similar to the system in Tibet whereby a new
Dalai Lama is chosen upon the death of the existing one.
Once the existing Kumari has reached puberty, she is rejected
from continuing as a goddess, as it is believed that the goddess
Taleju, a cruel and fierce manifestation of the goddess Durga,
has departed from the child's body. From this point on a new
child must be found whom the goddess Taleju can inhabit.

As soon as the existing Kumari reaches her first menstrual cycle, a great flurry takes place as priests have to find a new female child as quickly as possible. This cannot be just any child but only one taken from the Buddhist Shakya caste. When the news spreads that a new child is sought, mothers present their daughters to the priests, hoping that their child will have the honour to be chosen. Only children between the ages of 2 to 4 will be accepted, after which the rituals and tests can begin, which must be done very accurately in order to please the goddess Taleju.

First of all, they are presented to the astrologer and then examined for specific signs of the goddess. These include looking for required physical features as well as qualities of character and personality. There should be no physical flaws. She must have been in perfect health and never shed blood. Of the children selected at this part of the process, horoscopes are cast to make sure they don't clash with that of the king.

Once the child has been chosen by the priests, the next part of the process begins. One hundred and eight buffaloes and goats are sacrificed to the goddess Kali, and their severed heads are placed around the courtyard in the temple of Taleju. When darkness falls, the child is brought into the temple where she is left alone in the darkened chamber surrounded by the heads of the sacrificed animals. The only flicker of light is a gentle glow emanating from the *ghee* lamps, which are placed between the horns of the severed heads. After some time, the silence is broken by the beat of drums and the sound of rhythmic music as masked devil dancers with their twisted, contorted forms enter the dim light of the ghostly chamber. The priests, who are watching from a concealed place, watch to see that the child shows no fear or alarm at this part of the ritual.

After spending the night alone in the temple, the child is taken for her final test. Items of clothing and jewellery are placed on a table before her. Among these are possessions of the previous Kumari. If the girl child picks up the clothes and jewellery of the previous goddess, then the test is over, and the new goddess has been found. From there she takes part in one final ritual of cleansing, and all is complete. It is believed that at that point the goddess Taleju enters the child's body, and as the two become one, she becomes the manifestation of the Living Goddess.

Carried from the Taleju temple and across Durbar Square, she is taken to her own temple. Dressed in rich, red garments and opulent jewellery, and with a mystical third eye painted on her forehead, she is enshrined in the sacred place, which will become her prison until she reaches puberty. She will now be revered and worshipped as the embodiment of the goddess Taleju.

The area around the Kumari Temple was known to me quite well. I often walked past the entrance of the temple with its large, white stone lions standing guard at doors that stood beneath an arch of wood-carved human skulls. I'd also use the narrow alleyway which ran along the back of the temple, which acted as a short cut to Freak Street. This small lane joined with others that ran in a labyrinth of tiny passageways in a densely packed and populated area of the old city. Generations of people who had previously served the old royal family in the palace nearby, lived across this neighbourhood.

Most of the houses were in the old Nepalese style with intricately wood-carved doors and windows. The houses were packed together and were so old that some of the upper parts of the structure were leaning out towards the alleyway. Off the small, narrow passageways were small courtyards, which contained shrines to gods and demons. They were so tightly packed that the sun seldom reached the well-trodden paths below, and the cold and damp brought a stench through the narrow lanes.

As I walked along the lane behind the temple, I could almost touch the walls of the buildings on either side if I stretched out my arms. I would enter from the end near the Rat Temple, where rats were fed and worshipped on a daily basis, and walk along it until I reached the other end and came out at the place where Durbar Square connected with Freak Street. The narrow lane was lined with small open-fronted shops selling small plates of cheap fried meat and offal and locally made alcohol. Each one was dark and dingy and had walls and ceilings blackened from the soot of open fires and the dirt of many years. In the centre of the alley, large and imposing, was the back wall of the Temple of the Living Goddess. Its 250-year-old wall, like many of the other buildings in the area, leaned slightly outwards as if it was ready to fall.

Connected to the side of the temple was another old house with large, strong wooden doors facing out towards the alleyway. Entering through the doors, you would come into a small courtyard, which was surrounded by a three-storeyed house. On entering, you would be immediately confronted by a strong, pungent smell, which came from a small room on the right. Looking into the darkness of the room, you would discover a leather worker about his work. A small bed was pushed against the wall where he slept at night, and in the corner was a stove on which he cooked his food. Apart from a few pieces of clothing, hanging from a thin rope attached to the walls, there would be no other visible possessions. The strong odour, which permeated the courtyard, came from the leather that was being conditioned. The elderly owner of the house lived in rooms on the top floor, with his wife.

Climbing the narrow wooden stairs, you would come to three rooms situated on the middle floor. They were simply constructed, and the reddish-coloured floors were covered with dried mud and cow dung, a traditional form of insulation. Of the three rooms, one was dark and windowless and opened into the second room which contained a small kitchen and looked out over the courtyard. The third room was the largest, with a window which looked directly out to the opposite building as well as giving a view of the narrow lane below. With the sun unable to penetrate its windows, the house felt cold and damp and the smell of the leather and the lanes below seeped into its walls and interior.

There was nothing about it that was attractive, but it seemed like the perfect place for us. It was situated right in the very heart of Basantapur and was central to the people we wanted to reach in that part of the old city. We were offered the three rooms on the middle floor at a cheap rent and God provided enough for the first few months. We secured the rooms and set a date to move in.

Now, for me, a great step of faith had to be taken. As mentioned earlier, the Dilaram community provided food and accommodation and I had no other financial support. Once I walked out of Dilaram House, that was it. I had nothing, or no one, to lean on except God himself. I was hoping that God would have provided a steady, monthly financial income but right up to the day that I was to leave Dilaram, nothing materialised. The day came to depart, and I knew that this was a massive step of faith.

I also knew that faith often requires us to take a risk. I read Hebrews 11:8, which says, 'By faith Abraham, when called to go to a place he would later receive as his inheritance, obeyed and went, even though he did not know where he was going.' Sometimes faith requires us to take a step into the unknown, even when we are not sure where that step will take us. We may not always see the full picture or a way into the future. My journey so far had been like travelling with a flashlight. When using a flashlight, we can only see as far as the light reaches, but each time we take a step forward, we can see one step further ahead. I'd learned that if I did not walk in obedience to take the next step, I would never walk in the fullness of God's will for my life. I made my decision to launch out into the unknown. I didn't know how things would work out or where that first step would take me.

I continued to pray with the rest of the leaders and team in the Dilaram community concerning the new move I had felt God was leading me into. My time there had been enriching in so many ways. I had made so many new friends and had learned so many new things, but the day came for me to launch out into the unknown. After praying with the others, I placed my small bag over my shoulder. In it were the only few possessions I owned, which consisted of some clothes and a well-worn Bible. Then, following the familiar route, I walked under the jasmine tree and onto the street where I followed the dirt path across the rice fields and the rickety bridge into the old city where I headed for my new home. I had no idea what would happen next. All I had to hold onto was God.

15

A Church is Born

Claude and I moved into the apartment and began to pray for clear direction from God. Within a couple of days of moving in, I received a monetary gift which helped us to buy a few basic items we needed and which carried us through the next few weeks. I soon discovered that we were not alone in the apartment when on the first night I was woken from my sleep by a noise coming from the room that overlooked the court-yard. Heading into the kitchen area, I put on the light and discovered several large rats scurrying around the shelves and countertops.

Because it was a warm night, we had left the windows open without realising that this would be an open invitation for these unwelcome guests. We soon discovered that the Rat Temple created a large rodent population in the area. We quickly got someone to fix wire mesh over the window frames to stop the rats from entering as well as to keep out the nightly invasion of mosquitoes. This worked well at keeping the rats out, but didn't stop them trying to enter. Each night, for the next several nights, we listened to rats jumping up against the mesh and, in an attempt to hold on, they would dig their nails into the wire and, with a long scratching sound, slide down the mesh. They finally gave up.

Another noise that woke me up one night was the voices of men and women shouting below our apartment, in the alley. When I looked out of the window, I saw a group of drunken men and women fighting outside the house opposite us, and people going in and out of the front door of the building. The house was so close to ours that I could almost lean out of the window and touch it. That night we discovered that our neighbours were women involved in prostitution. What a great place to reach out to people with the good news of Jesus! With all that was going on in the area, we felt that we were living right in the devil's territory and prayed that God would use us to bring light into the darkness. It certainly was an interesting neighbourhood in which to live, as we were surrounded by drug dealers, hippies, pimps, prostitutes, criminals, home-brewed alcohol dens, ancient temples, an old palace and a living goddess.

We began to pray about how we could reach people with the message of Jesus. The question on our minds was how to do this in a nation where it was illegal. We knew that if we engaged in any kind of open evangelism, we could be imprisoned, or I would be deported. Either way, that would stop us doing what we felt God was calling us to do. Coming from the West, I was used to being in a nation where we were free to operate in any kind of open evangelism. Whether it was evangelism on the streets, hiring public venues, or using church buildings for evangelistic events, this was the usual way of doing things. We prayed for wisdom on how God wanted us to operate. I had read about the underground Church in places like China and knew that we would have to follow a similar pattern.

As I prayed, I felt God lead me to 1 Samuel 16 where I found the story of David being anointed as king by the prophet Samuel. God spoke to Samuel and told him to go to the house of Jesse and anoint one of his sons as king. Arriving at the

house, he asked Jesse to present his sons before him. Bringing
his first son, Samuel looked at him and thought this was the
one – maybe he was a big, strapping, kingly looking guy – but
God said, 'No'. Seven sons were brought before the prophet and
God gave his 'no' to each one. Being perplexed by the situation,
Samuel asked Jesse if he had any other sons. 'Well,' Jesse said.
'There's the youngest, but he's out looking after the sheep.' 'Go
and fetch him,' Samuel said. So, they brought young David before the prophet. The Bible says he had a 'fine appearance and
handsome features'. I think Jesse didn't present him to Samuel
because, maybe, he didn't fit the qualities of what he thought
a king should be. However, God had a different plan when he
said to Samuel, 'Rise and anoint him; this is the one' (v. 12).

Samuel was looking at the 'outward appearance', but God
was looking at 'the heart' (v. 7), and David had a heart that ran
after God's 'own heart' (1 Sam. 13:14; Acts 13:22). When the
prophet arrived at the house of Jesse, David was hidden from
him and he had no idea whom God would anoint as king.
Likewise, David had no idea that his meeting with Samuel that
day would change his destiny. God knew where David was,
and he led the prophet to him.

Through a totally supernatural experience, God pointed out
to Samuel the man whom he had chosen. Samuel anointed
David with oil, and the Bible says that 'from that day on the
Spirit of the LORD came powerfully upon David' (v. 13). In the
same way, God said to me, 'There are many "Davids" across
the city who are searching for me. I will lead you to them and
point out those who are open and ready to receive Jesus. Follow
the leading of my Spirit and go to those I show you.' So, in the
same way that God said to Samuel, 'this is the one' (v. 12), I
knew that, as we walked the streets in prayer, God would show
us the people whom he wanted us to reach.

Life went on each day as we settled into the area, and we began to walk the local streets praying that God would lead us to people who were open to him. The top of our house had a flat roof area, and as I had done previously, I would often climb the stairs onto the rooftop to pray. As I looked out over the rooftops of the old houses and pagoda-like temples, I would reach out to God in prayer for the neighbourhood, city and nation.

Some days, while there, I would look down to an open-roof terrace in the attached Kumari Temple and see the child goddess at play. Sometimes, catching my movement on the rooftop above her, she would look in my direction. She had been instructed not to smile at people, as it was believed that her smile would bring a curse upon those who witnessed it, even resulting in death. That did not stop me, however, from giving her a warm smile and a prayer from my heart. I always knew that, as our eyes met, she gave me a smile of acknowledgement with her eyes, and for a brief moment, while playing on her rooftop terrace, she was allowed to be a child again.

We continued to walk the streets, and God would lead us to people who were open to what he wanted us to share with them. Slowly, we began to see people give their lives to Jesus, and a small group began to form. I remember talking to a young Muslim guy one day. Approaching him, we struck up a conversation, and I invited him to our place for coffee. I spent the time sharing with him what Jesus had done for me; coming from a background where, to him, God was a God of judgement who offered little hope, he was emotionally moved by the fact that it was possible to have that kind of relationship with a loving God who cares. In ways like this, we met people on the streets and told them about Jesus.

So, we had a little group, and we would meet daily in an informal way to pray together, worship and study the Bible. Some of those who had become Christians had been small-time drug dealers who sold hashish to hippies. Now that they were Jesus followers, they knew that they had to change their profession. This created a gap between what they had been doing and finding some other form of employment, which meant they could not support themselves during that transition period. In order to help them, we took a few guys in to live with us. This meant placing blankets on the floor of the largest room to create a place to sleep; it also meant extra mouths to feed.

The monetary gift I had been given after we had moved into the Basantapur apartment was soon used up, and the day came when there was no money for food. We had eaten what had remained of our food supply earlier in the day, and as we approached the time in the evening when we would normally eat, there was still no food. This was a real test of faith. After praying, we decided to put our empty plates on the table in an act of faith and believe that God would fill them. As it got close to the time we would normally have dinner, we prayed and worshipped and wondered what God would do.

While we waited, there was a knock on the door, and as I opened it, I was greeted by one of the guys from the Dilaram community who had felt led to come and have dinner with us that evening. I smiled inwardly as I thought of the surprise he was about to receive. However, he went on to say that he hoped we hadn't eaten dinner yet, as he had felt that he should provide the food for that evening's meal. He handed me a large bag of food, and we had our miracle dinner. Our hearts were filled with gratitude for this provision of God, and it encouraged us to continue looking to him to supply our needs.

In ways like this, God continued to provide. Sometimes, while I was on the street, I would meet other missionaries I knew who would hand me envelopes containing money, saying that God had told them to give us a financial gift. These would always come at the right time. Other times, the money would run out, and people would invite us to their homes for food. We had the most incredible time seeing God provide, but nothing was as astounding as the time when, it seemed to all of us in the apartment, God multiplied the food.

We were down to our last few grains of rice, less than a handful of lentils and a few vegetables. We worked on a rota system for preparing dinner, and it was my turn to cook. There was not enough to make separate dishes out of the different food items, so we all laughed as I said I would just throw the whole lot in and hope for the best. What I put in barely covered the bottom of the pot, but I poured in some water, salt and spices, placed the lid on top and turned on the heat. After about ten minutes, I went to check that it was OK and saw that the lid was being lifted off by the food inside. I couldn't believe what was happening and called the others, who were equally astounded. Scooping some of the food out, I placed it in another pot, and it was enough to last for two days.

A few years ago, while I was in Claude's home in Darjeeling, where he then lived with his wife, we talked about what had happened that day. 'Did that really happen,' I asked him, 'or did I imagine it?' He walked over to the kitchen in his home and, reaching into a cupboard, pulled out an old, battered pot. 'Look,' he said. 'We still have it. We call this the "miracle pot", and every time we face a financial need, I take out God's "miracle pot" and remember that he is a God who can supernaturally multiply food and provide all our needs.'

One day I was walking across Durbar Square and sensed God was asking me to speak to a guy I saw in the distance. When I approached him, I discovered that he couldn't speak or understand English, and I couldn't speak enough Nepali.

Thinking that I'd misunderstood what God had said, I was about to give up when I felt God urge me to keep reaching out to this man. I couldn't figure out how I could do that but then had an idea. Our house was just behind Durbar Square and I knew that Claude, or one of the others, would be in the apartment. If I could get him there, someone would be able to share the gospel with him. Now a game of charades began as I tried to get him, through sign language, to follow me.

I think he must have understood what I was trying to say because he decided to accompany me along the alley and up the stairs into our apartment. I introduced him to Claude, and as we began to share our faith with him, he told us his story. He had come to Kathmandu from a distant village where desperate circumstances had overshadowed his family. His elderly father had a disagreement with one of the other villagers, which resulted in animosity between the two. In wanting to bring disaster on the family, the other man went to the local shaman and gave him money to place a curse on the elderly father. The guy whom I had just met on the street went on to say that, from that time on, his father went into a state of what he could only describe as insanity. He became detached, disorientated, violent, and his health rapidly declined. They believed he was demon possessed.

To try to remedy this, the family went to various shamans across the hills, giving them money to break the curse, but there was no deliverance or change. Their money now completely used up, they sold everything they owned, including a small piece of land, and came to Kathmandu looking for help. They now went to more shamans, doctors and hospitals and used up all the money they had brought with them, but the father became worse. The guy sitting across from us was now reduced to selling postcards on the streets to tourists in an effort to support his father, his wife and his children, who now lived in appalling conditions. He looked at us with desperate eyes and said, 'Can Jesus help my father?'

As he talked with us, I thought of one of my favourite stories in the New Testament, found in Mark 5:25–34, which speaks of a woman who had been 'subject to bleeding for twelve years' (v. 25). This is a story of Jesus stepping in when all else fails. She had been to 'many doctors and had spent all that she had' (v. 26), but no one could help. Reduced to what must have been a state of poverty and desperation, she heard of Jesus and believed that if she could just get to him, and even just touch his clothing, she would be healed.

Finally, her day of deliverance came. The news spread that Jesus, the miracle worker, was in town. Making her way through the streets, she heard the noise and saw the crowds in the distance. Believing that this was her day for a miracle, she did not let the throng of tightly packed people deter her but pressed through the crowd to touch the Master. Now she was close to him, and reaching out her hand, she touched his clothes. 'Immediately her bleeding stopped' (v. 29) as the healing power of Jesus entered her frail body. She knew that she was healed.

In verse 30 we read that Jesus asked, 'Who touched my clothes?' He looked around. He knew that healing power had flowed from his being. 'You see the people crowding against you,' came the reply from his disciples, 'and yet you can ask, "Who touched me?"' (v. 31). Then the woman looked into the eyes of the Saviour and confessed that she had touched his clothing. With love and compassion, he told her to 'Go in peace' and said that her faith in him had brought healing (v. 34). Jesus had done for her what no one else had been able to do.

As we told the guy before us the story of the woman who came to Jesus, we said that we believed God could heal his father. It was a bold statement, but we knew it was true. We asked if we could come and pray for his deliverance and healing. We agreed a time to meet the next day, which he said he would arrange at his friend's home. The next day we followed the directions he had given us and came to a simple, humble house, on the edge of the city, where we were warmly welcomed.

As we entered the house, the wife of his friend, who lived there with her husband and children, hurried excitedly towards us carrying a small book in her hand and saying, 'God has sent you. God has sent you.' When I looked at the book, I recognised it as a Gospel of John, one of the same books I'd carried into the mountains. She went on to tell us that several weeks previously, her daughter had been in bed, ill with a fever, and although she had given her medicine, she continued to get worse. In desperation, she prayed to God, and while praying, she remembered a book that someone from a new religion that she had never heard of before had given her. She remembered that the person who had given her the book had told her about a new god called Jesus who had great power. She'd never heard of this new god before but only knew of the Hindu gods whom her mother had taught her to pray to since she was a small girl.

As she prayed, she felt that she should take the book that contained the words of Jesus, place it on her child's body and pray to Jesus for her daughter's healing. Taking the book from a shelf, she placed it on her daughter's sick, feverish body and prayed to this new and unknown God. To her amazement, within the following few minutes, the fever had vanished and her daughter rose up from the bed completely healed. She then had a new prayer. She asked God every day that he would send someone to tell her more about this Jesus god.

When she heard we were coming she called some of her neighbours and friends, asking them to come and hear about a

God who had power to heal. Our new friend had brought his father, wife and children and we filled the small room at the front of the house, where we stayed most of the evening, teaching them about Jesus and the new life he offered. We ended with prayer, and each of them prayed with us to receive Jesus, and then we prayed for the elderly father. We broke the power of the curse over his life in Jesus' name and prayed for healing. As we prayed, a peace came over his whole being and his countenance changed. We knew that God had done something for him that evening, and the next day, his son came to tell us that his father was completely set free. In ways like this, we reached out to people wherever the Holy Spirit led us, and our small group of new believers continued to grow.

One of the new Christians in our group was returning home to his village in a remote area of Nepal, and asked if one of us would go with him to share the gospel with the people there. This involved a walk of around two weeks through the mountains to his village, which was near the Tibetan border in Western Nepal. As Claude spoke the language fluently, we decided that he should go, and I would stay in Kathmandu so that I could oversee what was happening there.

The day came when they set off on their journey. We gave them whatever money we had, which we hoped would be enough for the whole journey. Travelling through the mountains, they eventually came to the village, and after spending some days sharing the gospel with the people, Claude decided to return while the other guy stayed behind. He also left some of the money he had taken with the family, as he saw how needy they were.

After walking for a number of days, he came to a section of the journey that was very remote and prone to extreme weather conditions. As he pressed on, snow began to fall, and a sharp, cold wind began to blow around him, making it difficult to continue. By the time nightfall came, he had not been able to reach any place of habitation, and as the darkness closed in, he knew he would be left out in the open. As he kept walking headlong into the snow and biting wind, he was extremely exhausted and didn't think he would make it. Finally, he couldn't go any further.

Finding a small crevice in a rock, he tried as best he could to shelter, and lay down. Later, he said, 'The ground around me was covered with snow and I was so cold. It seemed like the freezing chill had penetrated through to my bones. I knew that I should keep moving but I was too exhausted. I thought that I would die.' As he lay there, he prayed that God would keep him alive and drifted off into a deep sleep not knowing if he would wake up the next day.

As he slept, he began to dream. In the sky above him he saw a large eagle descend from a clear blue sky, which was filled with the most glorious sunshine. The eagle continued its descent until it gently rested over him, and wrapping the large, soft feathers of its wings around his cold body, it filled his whole being with warmth. After several hours of sleep, as the sun began to rise and the snow and wind ceased, he woke up completely refreshed and ready to continue his journey. When he told us the story, we thought of the words of Psalm 91:4 which says, 'He will cover you with his feathers, and under his wings you will find refuge'.

After some days, the little money he had ran out, and as he passed through villages, he was unable to buy food. He had no other option but to trust God. Walking along a trail in a deeply wooded area, he was extremely hungry and asked God to provide something for him to eat. Journeying further along the trail, he came to a place where another path connected with his, and he was joined by an old Nepalese man who accompanied him some of the way.

After walking some distance together, the path broke off again onto another trail, which went in a different direction. At this point, the old man said he would be going on the other route, but before doing so, he reached into the folds of his garment and pulled out a round loaf of bread. Breaking the bread into two pieces, he passed half to Claude, and returning the other half inside his garment, he continued down the other path. Claude went on to tell us, 'I had never seen bread like that in any of the places I had passed through, and as I placed it in my mouth, it tasted so sweet. Even just putting a small piece in my mouth was enough to fill me, and it lasted for my final two days of walking.' He went on to say that he had wondered if God had sent an angel.

By now we had seen God do so many amazing things, and our little group of Jesus followers in Kathmandu had grown further. People were coming and going on a regular basis, and although some guys were still living with us, others had found employment and had places of their own. Added to these were others who lived around the area who had also become Christians. Up to this point, although we would meet with different people on a daily basis to talk, pray and study the Bible, we had no structured meeting where everyone would be together at the same time. Everything we did was informal and unstructured. We now wondered if it was time to start some kind of ongoing weekly gathering where we could all be together, and because everyone was from a totally non-Christian background, we could teach them more clearly about Jesus and how we should live for him as his followers. We would continue to keep this as unstructured and flexible as possible, allowing God to do whatever he wanted to do. Because neither of us had felt that we were qualified, or experienced enough, to be pastors, or even leaders, we never had plans to start a church. We were just two guys telling people about Jesus. I didn't really know how to preach or teach.

Saturday in Nepal is the one day of the week which is the official day off work across the nation, and because of that, we invited people to come to our apartment on Saturday mornings. We also told everyone we would continue meeting on that day every week. Saturday morning came, and as the room began to fill, people sat on the carpets we had spread out across the floor. There was an air of excitement as this was the first time we had all come together in this way. We started to worship God, singing some Nepali Christian songs; some of them were old, traditional hymns we had learned – these had been brought into Nepal from the Nepali-speaking areas of India – and others were English worship songs Claude and I translated into the Nepali language. After the worship I shared a message from the Bible, and before we broke up to drink *chai* and spend more time together in fellowship, we prayed, offering ourselves to Jesus to be his instruments of service in that land. It was at this point that I looked out across our humble gathering and realised that, without planning for it to happen, we had planted a church. And this was no ordinary church, it was a church planted right next door to one of Nepal's most powerful temples, the Temple of the Living Goddess.

16

More Miraculous Provision

I was reading my Bible one day when I came to the Gospel of Mark, and in chapter 5 it tells the dramatic story of a demon-possessed man who was set free from his condition by Jesus. The man who had received an incredible deliverance wanted to go with Jesus, but in verse 19, we read that Jesus looked at the man and said, 'Go home to your own people and tell them how much the Lord has done for you, and how he has had mercy on you.' When I read those words, they seemed to ignite something in my spirit, and I felt that God was asking me to return to England for a short period, where he would open doors for me to share with others what God had done. As I continued to pray, the desire in me grew, and I knew that this was what God wanted me to do. It was now autumn 1976, and I had been gone from the UK for two years.

We had been living in Basantapur for about six months and the church we had established was still in its infant stage, so I was concerned about leaving it, but by now there were others who could help while I was away. During my time in Kathmandu, I had become friends with some other missionaries from the US and India, and we had been meeting every Sunday evening to pray and encourage one another. God forged us together, and sharing the same vision and heart for Nepal, we became a strong team. I felt confident that all would be OK and that our new church would get the leadership, help and support it needed while I was away.

At that time, I met up with another friend of mine who was planning to return home to Scotland and wanted to take the overland route back to the UK. I shared with him that I was returning to England, so we decided to go together. As he was planning to be in India over the coming weeks, we decided to meet at Dilaram House in New Delhi and travel overland to the UK together from there. We set the date for when we would meet in Delhi, and I purchased a bus ticket that would take me from Kathmandu to the Indian border. I only had enough money to purchase my ticket to the Indian border and had no other money beyond that.

Day after day I was sure that somehow God would provide, but right up until the morning I was due to leave, there was still no provision of finances for me to make the overland trip to England. I actually wondered at times if I had misheard God and wasn't supposed to go. However, when I prayed, I felt a peace in my heart and knew that I should step out in faith. The day came for me to depart, and I packed some things into a travel bag. As I was about to leave the house for the bus station, Claude pressed some rupees into my hand. I actually thought God must have a sense of humour, as when I had arrived in India from Europe, all I had left in my hand was a few rupees, and now I was setting off back to Europe with the same amount.

I boarded the bus and we began our eight-hour journey down the winding mountain road towards the Indian border. After crossing the border into India, I purchased a second-class train ticket with the rupees I had been given, and headed for Delhi. I enjoyed travelling across the North Indian plains again, and it felt good to be back at the Dilaram community in Delhi where I was able to catch up with old friends. The rupees I had brought with me from Kathmandu were just enough to get me to Delhi. Now I would wait to see what God would do about the rest of the money that I needed for the trip to England. I didn't tell the guy I was travelling with that I didn't have the finances I needed for the rest of the journey.

We set a date to leave and I continued to pray. I had such a peace that God would provide, although I had no idea how. A few days before we were due to leave, as I was praying, I felt God say that there was some money waiting for me in a particular bank. He actually spoke to me about which bank the money would be in. The next morning, I made my way to the bank God had impressed upon me and located the department that dealt with overseas money transfers.

Walking up to the counter, the man behind the desk looked up from where he sat and asked how he could help. I said that I believed he had some money for me. He asked for my name and began to look through some papers that were in a container on his desk. After searching through them he looked back at me and said that he was sorry, but there was nothing under my name. Either he was wrong or I had got it wrong, but I felt sure that God had spoken. I said that I was sure he had some money there for me so could he double check. Looking slightly annoyed, he searched through the papers again until, with a note of surprise, he said, 'Oh, look, there is money here for you; there is £30 in your name.' Once again, I was blown away by another incredible miracle of God's provision. I now had the amount of money I needed to get to our next destination, which was Kabul, Afghanistan.

We took the train from Delhi and made our way across the Punjab until we arrived at the border with Pakistan. We then travelled across Pakistan by bus, which was a mind-blowing experience where I discovered that one of the national sports of Pakistan was bus racing – or so it seemed! The buses are colourfully decorated and are filled to capacity with people on the inside and piled high with goods (and sometimes more people) on the roof. At times, as we travelled along the road, a bus from behind would make an attempt to overtake. As it would draw alongside us, the race would begin, with our bus speeding up to try to stop the other bus from getting ahead. This was on a road which only had one lane running in either direction, so the bus trying to overtake us would face oncoming traffic. At this point, the windows of the bus being open, men and young boys would reach their arms outside the bus to beat the metal sides with their hands, loudly cheering for our driver to win the challenge. Just when it looked like the opposing bus was going to have a head-on collision with an oncoming vehicle, our bus would pull back to let the other bus pull in front of us.

After travelling through the mountains of Pakistan and ascending higher through the mountains of Afghanistan, we came to Kabul. It felt so good to be back in that city again, and we made our way to Dilaram House. We planned to spend a little less than a week there before moving on. I was looking forward to Sunday when we would attend Kabul Christian Community Church, which was now meeting in a house that stood on the ground that had been the location of the original church building.

Sunday came and I was excited to be in the church that held such a special place in my heart. While the service was going on, I began to think about how I would continue my journey and wondered how God would provide. In that atmosphere of worship, I told God that I trusted him. While those thoughts were going through my mind, it was announced that they would take the weekly church offering. I placed my hand in my pocket and pulled out the only single monetary note I possessed, which came to a few afghanis, the currency of Afghanistan. As the offering basket came towards me, I knew that although what I would be giving was a very small amount, for me it was 100 per cent of everything I had. As I gave my last currency note in the offering that day, I knew God would come through and provide all that I needed for the rest of the journey.

There were a few families still living in Kabul whom I had known during my earlier time there. One of them was Ray and his family, who were still based in Afghanistan. They invited me to their home after church that afternoon. It was great catching up with them and hearing of all that God had been doing through their lives and ministries. Ray himself had just returned from an overland trip where he had been speaking in churches in England and other parts of Western Europe.

As we were talking, he said he felt that God was asking him to do something. Turning to his daughter, he asked her to go upstairs and get all the money he had left over from their recent trip. Returning from England, on their way back to Afghanistan, they had unused money left over from each country they had travelled through. As they had planned to travel to Europe again at a later date, he had kept the money from each country for future use. After his daughter returned with the money, he said he believed God had just told him that it was for me. Once again, I was blown away by God's provision: with money in the local currency of each nation I travelled through, it was the exact amount I needed to make it to England.

As I arrived on UK soil, it felt good to be back home again, and after such a long time away, I enjoyed spending time with family and friends. As the news about what I had been doing in Nepal got out, I received invitations to speak in churches.

I thanked God for the opportunities he had provided for me to share about the needs of nations like Nepal and challenge people with the wider needs of missions around the world. As a result of this, I was now promised some monthly financial support which, although it was not a large amount, was enough to live on in Nepal, and it would be a regular income. I remember speaking at an evening meeting in a church where I was approached by a pastor who was attending the service. He said that the previous night, God had told him that he wanted him to financially support someone working in Nepal. He had never met me before and had no idea that the person whom he was coming to hear speak was working in Nepal.

It seemed that my time in England came to an end too quickly, and I could have stayed longer, but I wanted to get back to Nepal. I had been in the UK for a few months, and it was now time for me to return to the nation where more faith adventures with God awaited. I set my date to head back to Nepal and booked my ticket. This time I would fly.

17

Testimonies of God's Grace

I was so happy to be back in Kathmandu, and it was exciting to return to all that God was doing in the city. By now the church we had planted in Basantapur was well established, and we appointed a new leader to lead the group which was meeting there. Our team began to expand too. Claude had met Indira, a local school teacher who had given her life to Christ, and they were married. She was a beautiful woman with a passionate heart for God and for people. Then, another guy joined our team. Dilip had given his life to Christ in Basantapur, and it was clear that he had the call upon his life to serve God in a leadership capacity.

We moved to another area on the outskirts of the city with a vision to plant a second church. This time we were able to rent a house that was in its own compound. The house was a two-storey building, which gave us room to expand what we were doing. It was also situated among many more houses, which gave us contact with the people in the neighbourhood. We were excited to start something new here, and a few people joined us from the Basantapur church.

We began meeting each week in the large front room of the house. Once again, we kept everything simple. People sat on carpets placed across the floor, and the musical instruments we used for worship were an old acoustic guitar and a Nepalese *madal*, which is a long, round drum beaten with the hands. We started with a few people and continued to do what God had shown us, which was to walk the streets and pray that God would lead us to those who were open to him. One of the first people we met was a young man, somewhere around 20 years old, who was from the Sherpa community. We didn't realise it at the time, but our meeting with him would open a door into the large community of Sherpa people who lived in our area.

The Sherpas are a large ethnic group who mostly live in the mountainous regions of Nepal and have become known through-out the world for their work as mountain guides, especially into the Mount Everest area. They were originally a nomadic peo-ple from Tibet who migrated to Nepal several hundred years ago by making their way through mountain passes high in the Himalayas. Although not classed as Tibetans, they still maintain strong links with Tibetan culture and religion. Sherpas follow a form of Buddhism that is strongly influenced by the ancient Bon religion, which was in existence long before the arrival of Buddhism. Mixing the two together creates a religion which fo-cuses on mysticism, magic and a very real spirit world.

We discovered that the Sherpa people we would now be con-necting with believed in numerous deities and demons who inhabit mountains, caves, rocks and forests, and who must be constantly feared and appeased. These wrathful, fierce-looking, violent deities and demon spirits hold people in fear. If they are displeased in any way, they will bring curses upon the people. Propitiation of spirits, magic, blood sacrifices, rituals, spells, incantations, mantras, sacred arts and secret initiation rites are all woven into the lives, beliefs and practices of the people.

All of this is presided over by lamas (priests) but mostly by shamans, who are said to have the ability to expel demons and appease spirits and deities through various rituals. Shamans easily enter into visions and trances where, in their agitated and often frenzied state, they become the mouthpiece of gods and demons. We heard stories from remote mountain areas of dark spirits rising and appearing out of ritual fires, as well as other stories of supernatural manifestations, all of which could never be naturally explained. It was into this area that we were now about to bring the light of the gospel, and as we were to personally discover in an experience sometime later, the demonic power of Bon could manifest in a powerful and frightening way when confronted.

Looking for ways to make a living, many Sherpas had moved to Kathmandu where they found employment as carpet weavers. Each of their Tibetan carpets and rugs would be woven on looms, following ancient patterns. The rugs and carpets would then be sold locally as well as around the world. Finding accommodation in houses in our neighbourhood, they worked six days a week in workshops, where they would hand-weave the Tibetan carpets for which Nepal is famous. The guy we had just met began to visit us, and after a short period of time, he gave his life to Christ. He then started bringing others to hear the gospel, and as a result, we saw more people from the Sherpa community become Jesus followers.

One evening one of the Sherpas, who had recently become a Christian, came running to our house and asked us if we could come and pray for someone in the Sherpa community who was ill. We went with him into an old house, and climbing the stairs, entered a room that was filled with people. The room was darkened, and the air was choked with thick smoke from burning *ghee* lamps and incense, which was placed before a Buddhist shrine. On the bed lay a young girl in her late teens who was semiconscious. A Buddhist priest had been sitting on the floor before the sick girl for several hours, chanting mantras and reading sacred scriptures. In a slow, repetitive fashion, his low, mumbling prayers rumbled across the room. The whole atmosphere had a dark oppression.

Asking permission to talk to the group and pray, we told them the gospel message about Jesus and spoke of his power to heal. As they believed that the girl was under the power of demonic forces, we told them that Jesus had power over all evil powers and that when we know Christ, there is no need to fear. After we prayed for the sick girl, she immediately began to recover and within a few hours was completely healed and restored to health. This caused a further stir in the Sherpa community, and as a result, more people gave their lives to Christ and our group began to grow.

One morning I was in my room, which was on the ground floor of the house, when there was a knock on my door. When I opened it, a friend of ours who was visiting us from India, and staying with us for a few days, beckoned me to come with him up the stairs to the upper floor of the house. We had tried to share with him about Jesus, but he was a complete atheist with no time for God or religion. The reason why he had come to get me was because some people had brought a woman from a nearby village who was sick. When I entered the upstairs room, I found her lying on the floor clutching her stomach in severe pain. The man who had come to get me said we needed to get her to the mission hospital, which was close by, and offered to go and get a taxi. I was ready to do that but said to him that we would pray for her first. He said this confirmed to him that we were crazy and was one of the reasons why he was against religion.

Along with several other believers who were there, we gathered round the woman and began to pray in Jesus' name that God would heal her. As we prayed, the presence of God filled the room and a holy silence descended upon us. As we waited in his presence, the woman who had been writhing in pain now sighed with relief. As we had prayed, the pain in her body had subsided, and with a look of peace and joy on her face, she said that she was pain-free and healed. We lifted our hands to God and began to worship him and give thanks in his presence. When I looked around the room at the small number of people who were gathered, I saw the atheist with his hands raised thanking God with us. He said later that as we prayed he felt God's presence, and when he raised his hands he said something which he described as 'a gentle flow of electricity' ran through his body. He, along with the sick woman and her family, gave their lives to Christ.

Another young man, in his late teens, had been brought into the city from a distant village because of his need for medical treatment. He had been in pain and became partially crippled in one of his legs. This made it difficult for him to do any work, so he was becoming a burden to his family. Bringing him to the city, they took him to the hospital to see if he could be cured. The hospital did tests and told him he had an incurable bone disease and could do nothing for him. Even if they could have done something, the family were not in a position to be able to pay for the treatment he would need. Realising that his condition would get worse, and that there was no hope for him, his family decided to abandon him in the city rather than take him home where he would continue to be a burden. Now, left alone, he spent his miserable life begging on the streets of Kathmandu.

One day, as he sat by the side of the road in a poor and wretched condition, one of our church members approached him. Hoping he would receive a few coins, he looked up, not realising that he was about to receive something worth more than money. He was invited to church where he heard the good news about a God who loved him. As ragged and dejected as he was, he heard about a God who considered him of such value and great worth that he was willing to give his only Son to die for him. Out of so much rejection, he now found acceptance and love from a God he had never heard of before and from a community of people where he would receive care. Psalm 68:6 says, 'God sets the lonely in families', and surely, he had found a new family that day. He gave his life to Jesus and received prayer for healing, and from that day on, he grew to become a strong, healed, healthy young man who went on to marry, have children and start a small business in the city, where he became a wonderful trophy of God's grace. Jesus took a beggar and turned him into a businessman.

On another day, during the beginning of our weekly service, as we were worshipping God, a man entered and found a place to sit among the others. This was nothing new as each week people would join us. I didn't know who he was but found out later that, according to some of the church members, he was fiercely opposed to Christianity and he verbally, and sometimes physically, attacked those who became Christians, tearing up their Bibles and threatening them. His father was a prominent Hindu pundit (teacher) in the area who would attend religious gatherings where he was invited to read the Hindu scriptures and lead people in songs of prayer and worship to various gods. Knowing all this brought concern to those who knew him and were in the church service that morning, and they wondered what his intentions were.

Sometimes people felt that they had a prophetic word from God, which they would share with the group. This would happen when people sensed that they had a short message of encouragement that they believed God was giving them to share with those gathered in our worship service (see 1 Cor. 14:3,31).

I increasingly felt that I had a word from God that morning and began to share what I felt he had placed on my heart. The words seemed totally out of place for our gathering as I spoke them out. I said, 'As you have reached out to persecute, abuse and hurt my people, you have done it to me. Why do you attack me and reject me when I gave my life for you? I want you to know that I love you and I forgive you. Please accept my love and give your life to me.' There was a stir among the people as the guy who had persecuted Christians got onto his knees and, with tears running down his face, asked Jesus for forgiveness and surrendered his life to him. He suffered persecution and rejection from his father and the rest of his family, but went on to be a passionate evangelist sharing the gospel wherever he had opportunity.

In ways like this, God moved among us, and the news spread that there were some people who had brought a new religion which told of a God who loved them and had power to heal. People came to us for prayer, and we saw God do some of the most amazing things. We were able to share the good news of Jesus, and our group continued to grow. All this time we knew that we needed to be careful because of the laws against conversion, but it was becoming difficult to keep what we were doing quiet. This was especially true when we got to our first Easter Sunday as a church. All the new Christians were excited, as this was their first ever Easter Sunday when they would gather to celebrate the resurrection of the one who had given them new life. The day came and we gathered at the house. I counted around eighty people, and because there was not enough room inside, people were gathering outside at the front of the house. We opened the windows and doors so those outside could hear, and it was impossible to keep everything quiet. With great joy, passion and expression, everyone sang praises to Jesus, and the sound of their exuberant voices rang out across the neighbourhood.

Sometime after this, someone who had been visiting us told us that he felt that it was no longer safe for him to come. His cousin, who worked with the police, had told him that our house and activities were under police watch, and he went on to say that we needed to be careful. With this in mind, we didn't initially know what we should do. Not only were our lives in jeopardy, but we were also putting the lives of the other Christians at risk. Around that time, one of our team members, who had been visiting an area outside the city, was badly mistreated and thrown into the local prison for preaching the gospel. He was there for several weeks before he was released. We wondered if we should stop the gatherings in our house for a while and operate in a more underground fashion, or move the gathering to a different location. However, as we prayed, we sensed God telling us to continue as we were and that he would protect us. We continued and God did indeed protect us, as nothing negative happened to us.

Life continued to progress and our community of believers grew stronger. Most of our people came from extremely poor backgrounds, so we were not a rich church, but we all did what we could to help each other as well as help those outside the church. We took the words of Jesus seriously where he told us to love God, love one another and love those outside our church community (Matt. 22:34–40; John 13:34–35). Although we didn't have a lot of money, each week women in the church would take some rice, lentils, or vegetables from what they had at home and, pooling their small offerings together, would help feed the less fortunate. They found ingenious ways to help one another. If someone was pregnant, they would pull wool from old sweaters and knit clothes to keep the new baby warm through the cold winters.

Just like the early Church, our house churches had a strong desire and commitment to build community and care for one another. One thing I saw at work during this time was the power of faith. Many of the people who came to us were poor, and some came from impossible situations. What I saw was the power of a strong faith working in their lives that enabled people, through trusting God, to get through and climb out of any difficult, or seemingly impossible, situation. Time and time again we saw God make a way, and people progressed with their lives.

We continued to meet with our intercession group on Sunday evenings in the home of a missionary couple. Two more house churches had been planted in the city by others in our group, and our numbers were growing. At times, we would all come together. Christmas was approaching and we made the bold decision to gather all the believers from our house churches and go carol singing from house to house among their family members. We were all in agreement that, whatever the cost, we would spread the good news of Jesus through song and dec- laration. We all grouped together, and for several cold wintry evenings, we walked from street to street singing out the praises of Jesus and proclaiming the good news that he had come to earth to save humankind. These were exciting days, and as God was building his church in the city, he was getting us ready to take more bold steps of faith to reach people across the nation. However, as we moved into darker territory, this would involve confronting the powers of darkness head-on.

18

Confronting the Darkness

The second house church we had planted was becoming established, and although it was still early days, I felt that I wanted to move out to reach more people in new areas with the gospel, especially those outside the city where vast, mountainous areas continued to be unreached. With the Sherpas coming into the church, I listened to their stories of where, and how, they had grown up. I thought of the account of Jesus when people wanted him to stay in their hometown, but with a passion driving him on to reach more people he said, 'I must proclaim the good news of the kingdom of God to the other towns also, because that is why I was sent' (Luke 4:43).

I thought of the multitudes who had never heard the gospel, and as I listened to the stories of distant villages, my heart longed to go. Jesus knew what he was sent to do and only did what the Father instructed him. Likewise, we are all given different gifts, abilities and callings. God has designed us in a very unique way, so we are enabled to fulfil his specific call and destiny upon our lives. Knowing this, I wanted to stay true to what God was calling me to do, and by this time, I sensed he was asking me to reach more people with the gospel and plant more churches in unreached areas. The blessing of planting a church is that each one, when established, becomes a strong community for God in a specific area, which will stay long-term as a permanent witness of the gospel of Jesus Christ. When the church is planted and established in the correct way, and the right vision is birthed into it, it will grow and multiply into regions beyond itself. This became our experience as the churches we planted became established and moved from growth to multiplication.

All the Sherpas who were a part of the church came from Helambu, which is a mountainous region north of Kathmandu. Now that some of our people who had come from villages in Helambu had become Christians, they wanted us to take the message of Jesus to their unreached families and friends in the mountains. After much prayer, we decided that we should make some trips into these places and share the good news with those who were there. In each case this would take three days of walking, about twelve hours each day, along mountain trails to reach the villages. Initially, we would go and stay for up to two weeks and share the gospel with all who were open to listen to what we had to say. We would also pray for those who were sick and in need of God's touch of healing. It was on one of these trips that I was ill and had the experience with the shaman that I recounted at the start of this book.

One difficulty facing us was that the church was only six months old and it would be left for two to three weeks at a time. It was decided that Claude and I would go, and Dilip would look after the church while we were away, even though he had only been a Christian for a little more than six months himself. When he questioned our wisdom in this, we said that, out of all of the others in the church, he had been a Christian the longest. In the end, he did a fantastic job in leading the church and went on to become a prominent pastor and Bible teacher in the nation.

We now had a greater freedom to go where God led us, and while using the church as a base, we made some trips out to the mountain villages. This was a totally different world, where we were thrown back hundreds of years in time as we got to live in some of the world's most primitive, underdeveloped mountain communities, each one without electricity, running water or medical care. Life here is lived from day to day by eking out an existence from what can be grown on the mountainsides and eating only what each season provides. For those who own larger areas of land, things can be a little better. Life is generally one of tough survival, and thus the reason why many young people head to the city in search of work and a better way of living. However, these mountain people, although often poor themselves, will go to great lengths to show generosity and warm hospitality, doing the best they can out of the little they have.

We would walk for several days to reach each village and then would live among local people and tell them of a Saviour who loved them so much that he was willing to die to prove his love. We travelled light and trod the stony paths until we came to each destination. We would pass people on the way who were carrying heavy loads in baskets, or great bundles of firewood which were placed on their backs. I was surprised at the weight some of these people could carry, even at an advanced age.

It was in one of these villages that I experienced Tibetan tea for the first time. We had walked for three days and had arrived at a home in the village where we would be staying. The room was decorated in a typical Sherpa style. Wooden beds, which were covered with Tibetan carpets, were placed around the edges of the room, and in a place of prominence was the family shrine to local deities. The wooden window shutters were open to the sunlight and giving an incredible view across the pictur-esque valley. It was obvious that this family were a little better off than others in the village.

A plate of apples, freshly picked from the hillside orchard, were placed before us on the low wood-carved table and we were asked if we would like some tea. I couldn't think of any-thing more wonderful at that moment in time than a cup of hot, sweet tea. (Except maybe a hot shower and a comfortable bed!) By now I was used to the tea of Nepal which, like Indian tea or *chai*, is made up of lots of milk, sugar and tea leaves all boiled together in a kettle or pan and poured into a glass. I still make it at home today.

Chinese bowls were placed before us, and the tea was pre-pared and poured into the bowls. However, when I placed the bowl to my mouth and took a gulp of tea, instead of the sweet, milky taste I expected, it had a thick, salty, milky, rancid buttery taste. I didn't realise that Tibetan tea is made with salt instead of sugar and is sloshed together in a bamboo vessel with tea leaves, milk and a big glob of yak butter. I tried to hide my surprise and I think I did it well. I didn't really like the tea but knew that I should finish it out of politeness to our hosts. I quickly swallowed all the contents which were in my bowl when the lady of the house noticed it was empty and asked if I'd like more. I politely said 'no thanks' and she filled my bowl with more tea. I knew, again, that I would have to drink it. This hap-pened a third time and when I'd finished that bowl (they were large bowls) my friend leaned over and told me that leaving an empty bowl right side up signified that I wanted more. I quickly turned it over. I thought of the old missionary adage, 'Where he leads me I will follow, what he feeds me I will swallow.'

Another humorous incident I remember, though not hu-morous at the time, was when we needed to cross a river that, because we were at the end of the monsoon season, was in full flow. This time Claude's wife accompanied us as well as a Sherpa boy from the church who, although in his late teens, was quite small and thin. He was leading us to his village, which was still another two days' walk. We came to the river that needed to be crossed, but the waters were waist-deep and raging.

Some people from the village that was situated on the other side of the river said it was safe to cross, so we waded into the waters. I'm sure that for those sure-footed mountain people, who had grown up there, it was probably safe to cross, but for us city slickers it was a different story. About half way through the river the current increased in strength, and it was difficult to move forward. By now more people on the other side of the river had gathered to see the show and kept shouting encouragement. 'No problem,' they cried. 'You'll be fine.'

At that point, I felt that it was difficult for my feet to remain firm and shouted something to the other guys. Feeling the same way as me, the others in the river began to panic, and the Sherpa boy, who was convinced he would be swept away, wrapped his arms around my waist and held on tightly, refusing to let go. This made things worse for me, and I was sure that we would both go under the water, so by now I was struggling to get loose.

In her distress, Claude's wife, Indira, who was a few months' pregnant, began to pray out loud. Then Claude, like Moses of old who had parted the Red Sea, held out his walking stick across the raging waters and began to boldly declare, 'In the name of Jesus.' I think he was hoping that the waters would part and that we would cross on dry land. This all ended with most of the people from the village, who were gathered on the other side, bent over in laughter. They eventually gave us a warm welcome with lots of hilarity and pats on the back when we made it safely to the other side.

As fun as some of our trips were, we were never far away from the serious side of what we were doing, and nothing could have prepared us for an experience we had in one of the villages. As difficult as the lives of the mountain people are, they still manage to maintain an element of fun and happiness. However, behind all this, for them there lies a world of fear and deep superstition. As I mentioned earlier, gods and demons must be constantly appeased and one wrong move that displeases the spirits who live in the forests, rocks and mountains, can bring sudden, and lasting, disaster. The unseen realm of the spirits is very real to the people who dwell in the mountains and plays a major role in every aspect of their daily lives.

Claude and I were invited by one of the guys in the church to visit his village and share the gospel with the people who lived there. Again, we walked for three days until we reached his village in Helambu. He had sent word on ahead to say that we would be coming. Upon our arrival we were warmly welcomed by his family and were taken to a house which was made available to us for the ten days we would be there. The house was newly constructed, and the owners were away in India leaving it empty for our use, 'empty' being the key word as there were no furnishings of any description within its walls. The house was in the same traditional style as the others in the area. It had one room on ground level and an upstairs room, reached by a narrow wooden staircase, which had a wood floor covered with a heavy layer of dried mud and cow dung. In an area near one of the walls was a hollow in the floor where a fire would be built and the traditional rice, lentils and vegetables would be cooked. The smoke from the fire would rise upwards and find its way out though small gaps in the roof.

According to local belief and custom, at each stage of the construction of the building, a ritual would take place to invoke spirits to inhabit certain areas of the house. Each house should be inhabited by humans, animals and spiritual deities. The deities, or spirits, are invited into the house where they are said to take up residence, and it is believed that they will protect the home and its inhabitants from evil forces.

Our plan was to visit people in their homes and invite them to our house each evening where we would share the gospel. We would also visit those who were sick and offer prayer for healing in Jesus' name, thus obeying the command that Jesus gave to his disciples when he sent them out to preach (Luke 9:1–2). This would be done in an informal way, and we would explain who Jesus was and why he came, as well as the need to trust in him for salvation and new life. By sowing the seeds of the gospel, we hoped that, along with all of the other villages we visited, we would eventually see churches planted, which in turn would plant churches in the surrounding areas. Settled into the house, we rolled out our sleeping bags across the floor and slept.

The next day we prayed and asked God to guide us and use us in this village. Although the people were warm and welcoming towards us by providing a place to stay, at the same time we sensed some tension and resistance to the message we wanted to bring. Homes were not easily open to us, other than for the accommodation they provided, and although we invited people to visit us in the evenings, no one showed up. We continued to pray, sensing that there was spiritual opposition directed both against us and at what God wanted us to achieve while there. We also sensed that there may have been some opposition from the local shaman and priests, as we knew that they would not be happy with our presence in the village. This would explain why people were not visiting our house or inviting us into their homes. This went on for a few days as we continued to trust God and pray for a breakthrough.

One evening, after still seeing no change in the response of the people and no change in the tense spiritual atmosphere, we climbed into our sleeping bags and slept. Before sleeping, we finished cooking on the open fire, and because the room as well as outside the house was in darkness, we left the pans, tin plates and cutlery we had used on the floor at one side of the room until the next day. Each morning these would be washed from water collected from the mountain stream.

At the bottom of the stairs, in the room below us, was the door to the house that was the only entry. The room would usually have been inhabited by animals sheltering for the night, but in our case it was empty. As no one had been living in the house, there was no lock on the door, so one gentle push from the outside would cause it to open, giving anyone access at any time. On this particular night we were woken by the sound of the tin plates being shuffled around the floor accompanied by the sound of rapid breathing. Initially we were startled by the noise until we realised that one of the dogs, which had been untied at night to protect the village, had entered our house and climbed the stairs, discovering the plates and pans, which had remnants of food in them. We waited until the dog left the building and went back to sleep.

The next day everything remained the same. There was still no openness to our message and still no one came to visit us and, once again, that night we had the visit of the dog. The dogs kept in the villages are Tibetan mastiffs, which grow to a very large size and are trained to be quite vicious towards outsiders.

Again, the following day we actually wondered if we really would see the breakthrough we were believing for. However, that evening we did have a plan to deal with the dog. In the downstairs room we found a large, heavy slab of stone which we lifted and placed against the door which held it tightly shut.

We knew that a human would have the strength to move it, but not a dog. Feeling sure that the door was securely fastened, we blew out the oil lamp and went to sleep.

Like every other night we had closed the solid, wooden window shutters which protected us from the cold that descended upon the village every evening. This created a thick blackness across the room in which it was impossible to see anything, even at a close distance. We slept peacefully until, once again, we were sharply woken by the sound of a loud thud from the downstairs room, which alerted us to the knowledge that the stone slab that we had securely placed against the door had fallen. My first thoughts were that the dog had returned and I wondered how it had found the strength to dislodge the slab – but as I lay there, the thought crossed my mind that it could not be a dog.

We now listened cautiously to the creaking, raspy sound emanating from the door hinges as it was pushed open. Then silence. None of us spoke. Suddenly, the silence was broken as we heard the sound of human footsteps slowly, but steadily, moving across the downstairs floor. Next, we heard the creak of wood as a foot was placed on the stairs. Something felt wrong and I began to experience a strong feeling of fear and a sense of impending danger. I knew that there was opposition towards us, and the thought flashed through my mind that someone may have been sent to cause us harm.

By now we heard heavy, human footsteps coming up the stairs, each one pounding on the wooden stairway with a weighty thud. I immediately shouted to Claude to find the flashlight, which was placed on the floor between us among the other things we had brought for our stay. We searched with our hands in the darkness to the sound of displaced tin containers, falling candles and a knocked over oil lamp but, in our panic, could not find the flashlight. Although only seconds had gone by, it seemed like a long period of time.

As we searched for the flashlight, the footsteps quickened their pace and became louder, faster, heavier and increasing in speed. Now they were right inside the room. In the thick darkness we could not see anything but heard footsteps running in a frightening, frenzied fashion from one end of the room to the other. This way, then that way, then around the room. Thud, thud, thud. The choking atmosphere was filled with a thick, evil presence mingled with intense fear, and the noise of the footsteps got faster and faster with incredible speed.

At last Claude located the flashlight, and taking it in his hands, he pointed it out and clicked on the switch. As the darkness disappeared and light exploded into the room, the noise immediately stopped and we sat back in horror. There was no one there. The hair on the back of my neck literally stood on end. This was like something out of a horror movie. We both felt drained and exhausted.

Our next thought was that maybe there had been someone in the room after all, who had quickly retreated down the stairs and left the house. At this point, we were just pleased to still be alive and unharmed. We decided to go downstairs and check the room below. Using the flashlight as our guide, we headed for the stairs. Slowly and cautiously, we made our way down and prepared for danger or confrontation. As the light filled the empty space, we saw that there was no one present, and there, leaning against the closed door was the stone slab, exactly where we had left it. No animal or human had entered the house, and no one had left.

Going back up the stairs, we joined together in prayer. We knew that this was a spiritual attack. We had experienced spiritual attacks before, but nothing like this. The fight was on, the village was held in darkness, and we had to break it. We reminded ourselves of verses from the Bible. Jesus said to his disciples in Luke 10:19, 'I have given you authority to trample on snakes and scorpions and to overcome all the power of the enemy; nothing will harm you.' Then, in Ephesians 6:12, we find these words, 'For our struggle is not against flesh and blood, but against the rulers, against the authorities, against the powers of this dark world and against the spiritual forces of evil in the heavenly realms.' And 2 Corinthians 10:3,4 says, 'For though we live in the world, we do not wage war as the world does. The weapons we fight with are not the weapons of the world. On the contrary, they have divine power to demolish strongholds.' These verses, and others just like them, informed us of the fact that we were engaged in a spiritual battle.

We raised our voices to God and claimed total authority over the enemy, declaring the victory of Jesus. He said, when sending his disciples to the nations, that all authority was his (Matt. 28:18–20). We claimed that authority in Jesus' name and cried out to the God of breakthrough. Then, a miracle took place. The very next day, home after home was opened to us where we received invitations to share the gospel and pray for the sick, and evening after evening people came to our house to hear the good news. The powers of darkness had been confronted and Jesus had won the battle. The God of breakthrough showed himself mighty once again.

19

Permission or Prison?

We returned to Kathmandu full of joy at what had happened. The churches continued to grow, and we continued to reach out to new areas. After being in remote villages, I developed a burden for the thousands of other unreached villages across Nepal, and I constantly prayed about how we could reach them. I so desperately wanted them to know the gospel message that had so powerfully changed my life and was transforming the lives of millions of others around the world. Then one day, while in prayer, God spoke to my heart. Literature.

Up to that point, as mentioned earlier, the Bible was available in the Nepali language, and there were small portions of the New Testament available in printed form, but there were no gospel tracts which explained the good news of Jesus in a clear, simple way and which clearly communicated how a person could have a relationship with God through Christ. Although a vast majority of people in the villages of Nepal were illiterate, especially the older generation, I knew that there were many young people who could read and were hungry for literature.

The thought came to me, 'What if we printed tens of thousands of gospel tracts and distributed them far and wide across the nation?' Educational literature, and especially literature that is considered religious, was highly treasured and respected in Nepal and was given a special place in the home. I was sure that where people were illiterate, someone with the ability would read them out to family members and friends. Small pieces of literature could travel along every mountain path and valley and climb the highest peaks to the most remote village and hamlet. We could produce tens of thousands of little messengers who would spread the good news of Jesus. The excitement of this captured me in a big way, and I knew I had a word from God to do this.

Putting pen to paper, I wrote five very simple, clearly written, gospel tracts. Each one explained in different ways who Jesus was, why he came, and how we can have forgiveness, eternal life, and a relationship with God through him. At the end of each gospel tract was a personal prayer, which would help those who were reading, or those who were listening to what was being read, to give their lives to Christ and, through placing their faith in him, receive his free gift of salvation and new life. As soon as the five tracts were written in English, one of the guys in the church translated them into the Nepali language.

This was a very bold step to take in a nation where evangelism was forbidden by law, and we wondered how we would be able to print and produce the tracts. We thought of printing them in India, but then they would have to be carried into Nepal and go through customs checks. The only thing we could think of was to find a way to have them printed in Nepal. If God had told us to do it then he would provide a way to make it happen.

While we were thinking and praying about the way forward, the guy who had helped me translate the tracts said he knew someone who owned a printing press and might be able to help us. He had done some printing work for other organisations but never anything that was considered religious, and definitely nothing which pointed people to Jesus. After praying about it, we decided this was the direction God wanted us to take. Arriving at the printing company, we walked through the doors and were ushered into a room at the back of the building. The room was slightly dark and had a strong smell of printers' ink. Stacks of papers and files lay around the room, and in the background we could hear the steady, rhythmic hum of a printing machine at work. The man we needed to see was sitting behind a large desk and, inviting us to sit, asked how he could be of help.

We explained to him that we wanted to print some leaflets and had come to ask if he would take on the work. He glanced at the tracts we had produced and, without asking us what they were about, said that he would be happy to print them. We were slightly surprised that he said this so easily without checking the details of what we wanted to print. So far, everything was going to plan. We said our goal was to print 100,000 and would continue printing more after that. He said that would not be a problem. I thought to myself, 'This is going quite smoothly, almost too smoothly.' We settled on the cost of printing which, he said, we needed to bring on a specific day the following week to start the work. I told him that was fine, and that I would be there with the money. What I didn't tell him was that I didn't have the amount of money he had just quoted and needed God to provide it. Yet another time to trust God.

As we sat there, we thought of how easily this had gone and continued to be surprised at how effortlessly it had all come together. That was when he looked at us and said, 'OK, as soon as we get your literature back from the government, we can go ahead with the printing.' Government! We asked him to explain why it needed to go to the government. He continued, 'All literature must go to a specific ministry in the government to be censored and authorised before it can be printed. This is the law in Nepal.' We were not aware of this.

Now we both looked at each other, wondering what we should do. After all, this was a Hindu kingdom, with strict laws forbidding any kind of evangelism, and we were sending evangelistic literature to the government for authorisation to print 100,000 gospel tracts in their language, which would be distributed across the nation. At that point the thought crossed my mind that we should get out of there ASAP and find a plan B! However, as we quietly prayed, we sensed this was the right place. We thanked the guy behind the desk and left promising him we would return the following week.

We alerted everyone to pray. This was a first in Nepal, and we needed prayer cover for what we were doing. I still didn't have the money I needed for the cost of printing and didn't mention the need to anyone but kept it to myself and God. I was sure that if God had called me to do this, he would provide. As the deadline approached for our visit to the printing company, I still didn't have the money I needed. Then, a couple of days before we were due to go, I met a missionary lady at a gathering of friends. Before she left the group, she handed me a piece of paper and as she passed it to me, said, 'I felt God tell me to give you this.' She went on to say, 'I don't know why you need it, but I kept getting the word "literature".' When I looked at the slip of paper she had placed in my hand, I saw that it was a cheque for the exact amount of money I needed to begin the printing. This was so amazing, and my heart went out in gratitude to God. I thanked her and told her what I needed it for.

The day arrived when we were due to visit the printer. We prayed that morning before we went, not knowing what we would have to deal with when we arrived. Would we get to go ahead with our printing project, or would we be arrested? Would the outcome be permission, or would it be prison? We got out of the auto rickshaw and went into the building experiencing a mixture of both nervousness and faith at the same time. Thank God that, as we lean into faith, we find the strength and courage to press on with what we believe God has called us to do.

Walking into the office, we met the man we had spoken to previously, and after shaking hands, he ushered us to sit. So far so good. At least we hadn't been arrested yet. We waited with anticipation, wondering what the outcome had been. He went on to say that he had sent the articles we had wanted to print to the government ministry and these had been returned. Each piece had been looked at and checked and had been sent back to him signed and authorised for us to go ahead and print 100,000 gospel tracts. Wow! This felt like a major moment in history. We could barely believe what had just happened. We had been given permission to print and distribute 100,000 tracts that proclaimed the good news of Jesus in the Nepali language, in a Hindu kingdom, under laws which declared that all evangelism was forbidden. God had made the impossible possible.

Within the next couple of days, the great printing machine began to rumble and page after page of the good news of Jesus came off the press, each one ready to travel along ancient Himalayan trails. Everyone at church was so excited when the day finally came for us to pick them up. We brought back the first batch of literature and looked at the large quantities we had acquired. We prayed over them and asked God to use them to spread the good news of Jesus, and prayed for a great harvest in his name.

The next problem we faced was where to find the people to walk along mountain paths, and through hundreds of villages, to give out 100,000 gospel tracts. I was already committed to so many other things that were going on, and it was difficult to find anyone else free to go – and this was a lot of literature.

'Well, God,' I prayed. 'If you have provided the gospel tracts, and the money to print them, I'm sure you can provide the people to help give them out.'

A couple of days later, I received a letter from a couple I had met in India. They had been praying and felt that God had asked them to visit Nepal for six months, and they were to spend their time distributing gospel tracts. They asked if there were any available! Once again my heart went out in gratitude to God as I saw that when we trust him, and walk in obedience to whatever he calls us to do, he always works out the details. All we have to do is trust and obey.

The couple came and tens of thousands of tracts were carried along mountain trails and were given to thousands of people who had never heard the good news of Jesus. And the story doesn't end there. Over the following years more than three hundred thousand of these simple gospel tracts were translated into many of the different languages spoken across Nepal and were scattered like seeds across the mountains and valleys, bringing forth a bountiful harvest for God.

20

India and Beyond

If you take the main road used to travel from Kathmandu to India, you will cross the border and enter the Indian state of Bihar. This vast state, at the time I was there, had a population of around 65 million people living in tens of thousands of villages scattered across this area of North India. Here the land spreads out as far as the eye can see in a great flatness, which seems to stretch out in every direction forever. Through the land flows the great, majestic river Ganges, so wide in some places that it looks like a mighty moving ocean. Beyond all of this, the enormous evening sun descends, as it has done since the beginning of time, setting the endless sky ablaze with glorious fire.

During my time in Nepal, I had made a number of short trips into India where I would travel through Bihar and other North Indian states. Each time, I would be challenged by the great masses of people spread out across the land, the vast majority living in remote villages where life is primitive and extremely difficult. Bihar itself was always recognised as a wild, lawless state where poverty was widespread and people often took the law into their own hands. Whenever I travelled across Bihar by train, we would be accompanied by armed guards who would travel with us in order to protect us from bandits. These were the days when the infamous Phoolan Devi, the Bandit Queen, made famous through books and movies, was roaming the hills with her gang of outlaws.

It was now 1977 and I had been in Nepal for two years. I was praying one morning when God gave me a very vivid picture, which could almost have been a vision. In this picture, I saw a great mass of Indian people. The numbers were so great that I could not see where the crowd ended. Even today, the expression on their faces is still clear in my mind. Each one had a look of desperation and despair. Here were the ill and oppressed, the downtrodden and discouraged, the destitute and the broken, those who had no hope. The vision reminded me of the words of Jesus where he spoke of 'sheep without a shepherd' and he looked upon the people with great compassion (Matt. 9:36).

As I looked, I saw a great white dove hovering above the sea of people with its wings stretched out so wide that they covered the whole crowd. As the dove descended and moved over the mass of people with outstretched wings, it imparted hope, joy and life to each one. Every countenance changed as the dove brought love, comfort, hope and healing. I knew from the Bible that a dove represents the Holy Spirit. When Jesus was baptised, the Holy Spirit in the form of a dove descended upon him at the beginning of his earthly ministry (Matt. 3:16). I knew that the Spirit of God wanted to move across the land of India bringing salvation, hope and healing to millions of broken, desperate lives.

From that day on, God gave me an increasing burden to reach the masses of people in India with the gospel. I knew that I would continue working in Nepal but sensed God increasing my vision to move into wider areas and to preach to larger crowds. We always made it a priority in Nepal to raise up local leaders, let them help make decisions and be involved in the leadership of the churches. We had a great team of leaders in Kathmandu now, and I felt freed up to travel and focus on itinerant evangelism. That said, I always wanted to give priority to church planting. I didn't know what the next step would be, so I left it all in God's hands. I actually could not see myself preaching to larger groups of people, as this was something I'd never done before. I didn't really consider myself to be a preacher or evangelist.

I shared what I was feeling with a few others and asked them to pray. Several weeks later one of the people I had told was visiting Chennai, South India where she met a pastor who was planning to plant a church. He informed her that he was looking for an evangelist who would be available to visit his town and preach at an evangelistic event which would kickstart the new church. He asked her if she knew of someone who could help. She said she knew just the person and gave him my details. Shortly after their meeting, I received a letter of invitation to go and preach. This was something totally new to me and I was unsure. However, I wrote back and told the pastor that I would come. I knew he didn't have financial resources to fund the event, so I told him I would finance the whole thing, which for me was another step of faith.

We fixed a date and I arrived in Chennai, with two others who travelled with me, and met the pastor. Miraculously the money to fund the event had come through. We hired the use of a large open public ground in the centre of town where we built a stage and set up some lights and sound equipment. We then printed, and distributed, thousands of flyers inviting people to the five-day event, which would run from Wednesday to Sunday. The first night came, and I have to admit, I was slightly nervous, wondering if people would actually show up. The singers were in place and the sound and lights were switched on, but there were very few people scattered across the grass. Then the worship team started singing, and people began to gather, and in the end we had around seven hundred people attend on the first night. To me it could have been 7 million as it looked such a big crowd.

I sat on my seat waiting for my time to speak. I had several thoughts going around in my head on what I should say, but couldn't settle on anything in particular. I could feel the pressure building and wondered if I had actually done the right thing by coming. I looked out at the crowd of people and saw that every one of them was special to God and had come that evening looking for a message of encouragement and hope. As I looked at them, I prayed and said, 'God, please give me the right words to share with these precious people.' And as I sat in that open ground, which had become a dwelling place of God, I heard him say, 'Tell them I love them.' And that has pretty much been the message which has guided me in my ministry over all these years. People need to know that God loves them and that they are precious and valuable to him.

I smiled inwardly when the pastor went to the microphone and said, 'And now we invite international evangelist Geoff Walvin to preach God's Word.' International evangelist! I think the biggest crowd I'd ever spoken to was about eighty people and that seemed like a big crowd to me. I was amazed that everything had come together so well so far. In the end we had the most wonderful time, as night after night the numbers increased, and people gave their lives to Christ, and after receiving prayer, many gave testimonies to say that they had received healing. And that week a new local church was born.

My heart was stirred to reach more people with the gospel, and I saw this as an effective way to start more new churches, especially in areas where open evangelism was allowed. By working with local people, I saw the potential in church planting by using this method to gather people, share the good news, and leave a team behind to lead and establish a new church. I thought of the vast unreached areas of North India where, unlike South India, the Christians were a very small minority of the overall population. I thought of places like Bihar with its thousands upon thousands of towns and villages with no church and no one to tell them the good news, and I sensed God was moving my heart in a new direction.

On the last evening, I was approached by a man who had attended the event. He introduced himself and said that he was the director of a newly formed ministry that was reaching people in North India with the gospel. As we continued our conversation, he asked me if I would be willing to go and preach for them in evangelistic events that would help them plant churches in unreached areas of North India. They had recently sent a team of local missionary workers from South India to the north with the goal of evangelism and church planting. I asked him where in North India, and he replied, 'Bihar.' I instantly knew that this was God at work. This divine appointment, with a total stranger, launched me into an exciting, adventurous, powerful ministry in Bihar that would almost cover the next two years.

I immediately made contact with the team in Bihar, and we began to make plans. This worked out well, as I could continue working in Nepal while crossing the border to hold evangelistic events in Bihar. I was reminded of the account in the New Testament where, in Luke 5:4–7, Jesus encourages Simon Peter to launch out into deep water and throw out his nets for a catch of fish. Simon Peter replies, 'Master, we've worked hard all night and haven't caught anything. But because you say so, I will let down the nets.'

At that, he cast his nets out into the deep and the results are amazing. He catches such a large amount of fish that his nets begin to break and the story goes on to say, 'So they signalled to their partners in the other boat to come and help them, and they came and filled both boats so full that they began to sink.' By working with other people, they were able to bring in a greater haul of fish, but before that could happen, they had to launch out into deeper waters. I definitely felt that God was calling me out to deeper waters and to a place of ministry to which I had never been before. What God was asking me to do would require more faith, more finances and more commitment to a wider vision and ministry. I also saw that by partnering with others, we could bring in a greater harvest. It was now time to move into a wider itinerant ministry in which, by partnering with local pastors and church planters, we could achieve so much more.

As I prepared to launch out into deeper waters, I could be assured that the same Jesus who was with Peter when he walked on the water was with me and would not let me sink (Matt. 14:22–33). Sometimes, in order to move forward and progress with our lives, we have to take the scary step of launching out into the unknown, being assured that the God who calls us has promised to never leave us or forsake us (Heb. 13:5). He will be with us every step of the way. The meetings in Chennai had opened my eyes to a whole new vista, and I wanted to see this replicated across India.

Within months I was conducting my first evangelistic event in Bihar. I worked closely with the team of Indian missionaries who had left their homes in South India in order to share the message of Jesus with those who had never heard in the north. The strategy was simple. They would choose a town, or city, where they wanted to plant a church. I would then go in and speak at a five-day evangelistic event, beginning on Wednesday evening through to Sunday evening, then on Sunday mornings we would have our first service to launch a new church. In each place, team members would be left behind to lead, grow and establish the new church.

I travelled across Bihar and preached the gospel to thousands of people who had never heard the good news of Jesus before. Focusing on cities and towns, we proclaimed the message of hope and salvation in open, public grounds, and in every place, we saw the supernatural power of God at work to bring healing and deliverance, which resulted in many people giving their lives to Christ, and new churches were planted. Building on the blood, sweat and tears of missionaries who had laboured before us, their ancient prayers saturating the land, we reaped where they had sown.

For almost the next two years my time was divided between Kathmandu and Bihar. My time in Kathmandu was now spent in preaching and teaching in the churches, which were growing as more people were becoming followers of Jesus. During this season we began to spend more time in teaching and training future leaders. The churches were becoming more missions-focused, and they were catching a vision to plant more churches across Nepal. Requests were now coming in from far and wide, as people in towns and villages wanted someone to come and share the gospel.

Across Bihar, which at that time was called 'the graveyard of missionaries', we went into some of the most difficult, hard to reach areas where Christians were almost non-existent. We went to one town where there were a group of seven Christians who met in a small building attached to one of their homes. They faithfully met there to pray for their town and surrounding region. When they knew we were coming, they offered to help and said we could use their small building as a base for a future church. They had been praying for a pastor and longed for a move of God across their town.

We began the event in a public place, which was well attended, but at the end of the second evening's meeting we were approached by the police, who ordered our meetings to be closed down. They assured me it was for my own safety which, as they said, they were responsible for. Some hard-line religious elements had threatened to create riots, disrupt the event and physically attack us if we did not stop what we were doing. I said that we were prepared to take the risk and continue with the meetings, but the police informed us that if we decided to continue, they would place the whole town under curfew each evening. We were not even given permission to come the following evening to let people know the event was cancelled. We decided we would wait until Sunday, have a small service with the seven Christians in their building on Sunday morning, and leave the town after that. Sunday morning came, and as we arrived for the service, we were amazed to find not seven people but around seven hundred people waiting for us. They spilled out across the compound and onto the road. We had a powerful time that morning and saw, once again, many people give their lives to Christ.

God did amazing things during that period and showed himself mighty to help us, even in times of opposition. In one town, we had hired a public ground in the centre of the town for five evenings. We advertised it widely, inviting people to come. The lights and sound system had been set up the day before, and we were ready to begin the event the following day.

On the next day we arrived in the afternoon to make final preparations for our first meeting that evening. While there, we discovered that someone had rented a small hall on the site of our ground for a clothing sale, which would be open through-out the day as well as every evening while we were there. To advertise the sale, the salesman was playing very loud, high-pitched Bollywood music through a powerful sound system. This created a problem for us, as the sound of his music would negatively clash with our singing and preaching, making it difficult for people to concentrate and clearly hear what we were saying. It would be total chaos. We asked him if he would be willing to turn his music off while we held our meetings each night. No matter how much we tried to talk to him, he steadfastly refused. We decided to pray and trust God.

It was approaching 6.30 p.m. when we had advertised our meetings would begin. People began to gather while his music was still blasting out the latest movie songs. Darkness was quickly descending on the town and our lights shone brightly across the ground. It looked like an impossible situation. The time arrived when we were due to begin, and we looked at each other, wondering what we should do. Suddenly, there was a power cut which plunged the whole town into silence and darkness. In an instant, the clothing sale music stopped and his hall, like the rest of the town, was plunged into darkness. It just so happened, however, that we were operating our event off our own electrical generator, so we were not dependent on the town's supply. We were the only place in town with light and sound.

The clothing sales man came and asked if he could run an electrical cable from our generator to light up his hall. We helped him light up his business, and he was so grateful that every evening, promptly at 6.30 p.m., he switched off his music. The other plus side that first evening was that the town, with no electricity, was in total silence except for the preaching and testimonies of healing which echoed out from our sound system. They had no other choice but to listen. This brought an even greater crowd the second evening, and God did some incredible things.

Night after night, in town after town, we witnessed the power of God manifest in awesome and miraculous ways. Often, people would travel in from surrounding villages to hear the good news and receive prayer. At one event, people who had come from thirteen outlying villages decided to become Jesus followers, and as a result, our teams were able to establish house churches in each of these places. In ways like this, the kingdom of God became established in hearts, lives and homes across the region.

During the 1970s a movement swept across Bihar which became known as the Naxalite movement. The Naxalites were influenced by communism and were committed to take from the rich and give to the poor, by robbery and violence if necessary. Because Bihar was plagued by poverty, many young people were drawn into this movement.

One evening, when we had concluded our meeting, we were approached by a group of around a dozen young men who had heard that we were preaching about Jesus and had travelled from their village to come and find out more. I noticed one of them had two large scars along the left side of his face. The youngest in the group was 12 years old. A young man from the group, whom I recognised as the leader, shared his story with us. A few years previously, a man who was heavily involved in the Naxalite movement entered their village. It turned out that he was a fugitive who was wanted by the police for murder and robbery. The young man had taken this fugitive into his home and had given him shelter. The end result of this was that the group before us were indoctrinated into the Naxalite movement in which they became actively involved.

As they talked, they shared with us their frustration and regret of how they had been living and wanted to be set free from lives that were filled with hatred, violence and crime. They went on to say that they wanted to become followers of Jesus. As we led each of them to Jesus that night, we witnessed the power of darkness over their lives broken, bringing freedom, forgiveness and redemption. They then invited us to come and share the good news with their whole village.

Our jeep shuddered and shook along the dusty, dirt road as we approached the village that had been a Naxalite stronghold. As we approached, children waved at us from the roadside, and we received a warm welcome as people gathered to greet us. For two nights, standing in the centre of the village surrounded by buffaloes, cows, bales of hay and mud houses, we shared the good news of Jesus with several hundred people who were open to the gospel and the power of God. Before leaving, we taught, preached, prayed and baptised in the nearby river, and what was once a Naxalite stronghold now became a beacon of light for the kingdom of God.

From there, I began to travel across India as invitations came in to preach at various places from north to south. I continued to be based in Kathmandu and helped with the churches there between making trips into India. Due to the different needs in various places, I added teaching to my regular preaching. Each morning, in our evangelistic events, we added teaching sessions, which were always well attended. As all of this was developing further, we added leadership training as we saw the need for future leaders.

In Kathmandu we set up weekly teaching and training for those who felt called to leadership. By now, I was travelling a lot and was often on the road for two months at a time speaking at evangelistic events, churches, conferences, training schools and seminars. As I moved across the length and breadth of India, I would usually travel by train on journeys that would sometimes take two days to complete. This would always be in open, second-class compartments, which were often filled to capacity. Here I would share life with hundreds of others as each train, packed with people, noise and life made its way across this great land like a moving Indian village on wheels. Then, added to this, God began to open doors for ministry into other nations around the world. This would take me to Bangladesh, the Maldives, Malaysia, Singapore, Brunei, Japan, Mauritius, Holland, Denmark, Sweden and the US. These were busy but powerful and fruitful days where God did so many incredible things that the stories would fill another book.

In 1986, I sensed God asking me to move my base to New Delhi. A team from a church in Singapore, led by Connie Ong, had been in New Delhi for several months where they had planted a church. As the team were leaving to return to Singapore, they asked if I would be willing to lead the new church and outreach. After spending some time in Singapore, I flew to New Delhi with a team of young people. We had specific ideas of what we wanted to accomplish while there, but God had a plan that was beyond anything we could have imagined.

We held services each Sunday in the house in which we were based and used the large front room for weekly gatherings. Throughout the week, the team was involved in personal evangelism on the streets. This was frustrating, as we were unable to make much headway and saw very little response. However, we kept on praying and believing God for breakthrough. One day there was a knock on the door, and when I went to answer it, I was met by two young men who said they wanted to know about Jesus. They were from a Muslim background and had come to India from Iran. After the Islamic revolution in Iran in 1979, many Iranians who supported the Shah had fled the country because of often severe and brutal persecution and sought refuge in other nations. I invited them in, and we talked over tea. After a lengthy conversation, they both gave their lives to Christ and joined us for church the following Sunday.

The Sunday after this they brought six more people to church, all from Muslim backgrounds. At the end of the service, five of them said they wanted to give their lives to Christ. I wasn't sure if they fully understood what the social implications of this would be for them, so I explained again what all this meant. They said they understood and wanted to become followers of Jesus. After this, Sunday after Sunday, for a period of six months, people from Muslim backgrounds came to hear God's Word and give their lives to Christ.

Some of the most powerful things took place during that period which caused many of them to turn to Christ. Most of them were from Iran, with a minority coming from Afghanistan and Iraq. I thought of the prayers I had prayed earlier while in Afghanistan and travelling through Iran and felt so blessed to be among these precious people. We moved the church from the house to a larger hall and had wonderful meetings week after week where people shared powerful testimonies of answered prayer. The church consisted of around eighty Muslim-background believers as well as other local people who had joined us.

One of the women who had become a Christian was married to an Iranian who had a strong position of influence over the Iranian community in India, which numbered several thousands. He came to visit me one day and, as we drank tea together, said he had come to thank me and to say that the whole Iranian community was open to me sharing the gospel, because, as he said, 'You have given my people a wonderful message which has given them hope and has changed their lives.' I never saw any outward evidence of him becoming a Christian, and he never did attend church, but he saw the power of hope in the gospel to change lives. We had wonderful times back then where we would all meet and share life together day after day.

The churches continued to grow and multiply and the number of people becoming followers of Jesus continued to increase. It was now 1990, and I had been in India and Nepal for fifteen years and began to sense that my time of living here was coming to an end. These years had been filled with challenge and adventure. I had taken some faith-fuelled risks. I had learned a lot, experienced a lot and grown a lot during this time. Above all, I had made rich, lasting friendships and my relationship with God had grown in so many ways.

By now I had learned that when one season of our life comes to an end another season begins, which can be filled with just as much wonder as the last one. I felt that God was leading me to return to England, the land of my birth. This created a sense of sadness because, although my connections with India and Nepal would remain strong, I would no longer be living in that part of the world that I had grown to love, and which had enriched my life in so many ways.

I looked out of the window of the plane and saw the green fields of England spread out beneath me. The plane came to a halt, and I reached up into the overhead locker and took out the small bag that contained the few possessions I had brought with me. The door of the plane opened, and with great anticipation as to what would come next, I stepped outside ready for a new season and a new adventure with God on this incredible journey of life.

Epilogue

Since leaving India some thirty years ago, I have made my home in the UK. I have always kept in contact with many of the people I came to know in the early days of ministry in India and Nepal, some of whom became Christians during that time. Today many of them are prominent leaders in churches and Christian organisations. The few churches we originally planted in Nepal have continued to grow and multiply, through the hard work and sacrifice of brave men and women, to a movement of around 1,200 churches today. They have also developed one of Nepal's leading Bible schools, which trains and sends out people every year to serve God in church leadership.

Some of the original house churches now have congregations with attendance numbering into the hundreds. Many of the young people who became Christians in our early days are now nationally known leaders with solid, established ministries in Nepal. The number of Christians in Nepal today is estimated to be around 1 million, but some local church leaders would put that closer to 3 million.

Our first, small Easter Sunday gathering, which took place in the early days of our house churches, seemed like an amazing thing to us. Today, every Easter Sunday, thousands of Christians march through the streets of Kathmandu in a wonderful display of vibrant worship and proclamation of the risen Christ.

The team I worked with in Bihar, where we planted several churches, have continued to work for God, and the original churches have grown and multiplied until there are more than 1,000 churches there today. Many other ministries have been established which reach out to some of North India's neediest people. Like the churches in Nepal, they have developed a solid training school, which sends out workers every year.

The Iranians and Afghans who made up our Delhi church have been resettled in different parts of the world. I'm still in touch with some of them.

On one of my previous visits from Nepal to the UK, I looked across a church one evening and saw the woman who I knew would one day become my wife. She introduced herself as June and we got to know each other during my short time in the UK. Distance kept us apart, but we kept in touch for several years, and on my return to England, we developed our relationship further. On a beautiful day filled with glorious sunshine radiating from a clear blue sky, we walked down the aisle together and pledged our love to one another in marriage. This beautiful woman became my partner, soulmate and the love of my life and we set out on a journey together to serve God and reach out to help others. In time, we were blessed with two wonderful daughters, who have grown to be beautiful young women, and of whom we are so proud.

For a few years I was on the leadership team of a local church while continuing with itinerant ministry in the UK and overseas. While praying one day, my wife and I felt that God was asking us to plant a church in the north of England. I still maintained a heart for South Asia, and we were blessed to see the church we started grow and develop into a multicultural community that also included people from India, Pakistan and Sri Lanka. We maintained a strong connection with the local South Asian community.

We built bridges into the Hindu and Muslim communities during this time, where we established friendships with many wonderful people, many of whom attended our church events. The church developed into a strong family where, as people of different races and cultures, we would share life together. Our international lunches became popular and attracted many people, and there was always an abundance of hot, spicy food! I led the church we had planted for twenty-three years, until I stepped down from leadership two years ago. Throughout this period, I continued to make ministry trips overseas, something we plan to continue.

Missions is still important to us, and although the church is making great strides in many parts of the world, there are still vast areas where millions are unreached with the gospel. Let's continue to pray for these needy areas and please pray for the church in India and Nepal.

In thinking about my story, I'm reminded that we all have a story to write. Thank you for reading mine. I hope it has blessed you. For each of us the journey has not ended and each day is a new beginning. There are still pages to be written in the book of our lives and I pray that yours will be filled with the amazing wonders of God. May you write it well.

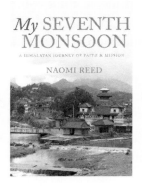

My Seventh Monsoon

A Himalayan journey of faith & mission

978-1-86024-828-3

No Ordinary View

A season of faith & mission in the Himalayas

978-1-86024-843-6

Heading Home

My search for purpose in a temporary world

978-1-86024-853-5

A trilogy of books from Naomi Reed, describing her life and work as a missionary in Nepal alongside her husband and young family.

Blood, Sweat and Jesus

The story of a Christian hospital bringing hope and healing in a Muslim community

Kerry Stillman

What is a Christian hospital doing in a remote Muslim area of Cameroon?

Kerry Stillman shares her own experiences of working as a physiotherapist in a sub-Saharan village hospital. A vivid impression of daily life is painted as the team deal with the threat of terrorism, the attitudes of local people towards Western medicine, their patients' health issues, and the challenge of sensitively sharing the gospel in a different culture.

Passionate, intriguing and uplifting, this is a colourful interweaving of cultures, beliefs and the power of prayer alongside modern medicine.

978-1-78893-148-9

Authentic

We trust you enjoyed reading this book
from Authentic. If you want to be
informed of any new titles from this author
and other releases you can sign up to the
Authentic newsletter by scanning below:

Online:
authenticmedia.co.uk

Follow us: